Not Religion
but Love

Praise for Dave Andrews

One of the leading prophetic voices of our times.
Mike Riddell, *Godzone*

Writes with a wealth of experience on matters dear to my heart.
Jim Wallis, *Sojourners*

A deep thinker who has a rare gift of interpreting the activities and motivations of [the] society where he finds himself.
Mike Feeron, *Christian Week*

He is offering more than a practical sound bite. With Dave Andrews, theory has become practice, and truths take on a life of their own.
Simon Mayo, BBC Radio 1

This English-born Australian-sounding father of two is really a kind of urban peace guerrilla!
Clive Price, *Christian Family*

Dave is ordinary, but believes ordinary people should take extraordinary risks to confront the cruelty in our world!
David Engwicht, *Eco-City*

People like Dave could be branded 'radical' and be shunned ... But he does not harangue people. He provides [us] with suggestions to help us look at our communities.
Irene Oliver, *Queensland Baptist*

Dave has a calmness that radiates serenity [and] a warm human understanding.
Ranjan Gupta, *Sydney Morning Herald*

Very practical, compassionate, and empowering.
Trevor Jordan, *Dayspring*

Dave Andrews has long excited our admiration for his work with marginalised people. Dave makes us ask [ourselves] if we can build a better world. If there were more people like Dave, and his partner Ange, to inspire us, we would be able to reply with a resounding 'Yes!'
Charles Elliott, *Signs of our Times*

Praise for *Not Religion but Love*

Not a book comfortable Christians will enjoy, but one they should read!
David Penman, late archbishop of Melbourne

This is one of the most easy to read, yet hard to read books that I have picked up in the last few months. It is easy to read because it is simply written in a very easygoing style. It is very hard to read because it challenges [our] values, [and] asks us to demonstrate Christ-like commitment to those in society that are hurting that [is] personally costly.
Peter Kaldor, *On Being*

(This book) has a profound down-to-earthiness. It's not about dropping *out* of society, as it is dropping *into* society. It opens the door to effective human care by the ordinary person with ordinary skills, and a caring heart. The commitment to real care (it communicates) is extremely powerful.
Trevor Roper The Daily Sun

Dietrich Bonhoeffer's Cost of Discipleship provides a powerful challenge to follow Christ in our world. Dave Andrews shows us *how* we can follow Christ in ways that serve the community.
Charles Ringma, Professor, Regent College, Vancouver, Canada.

There is a genius to this book in the way it has been written. If you are looking for quotes, the powerful punchlines come thick and fast. At the end of each chapter is a section for ideas, meditation, discussion and action, which makes it a great tool for . . . living prophetically as people of hope. It is not a book that compounds guilt, but it cleverly takes us to the point of no return where action must follow obedience into ministry to a hurting society.
John Uren, *Target*

A good many are committed to social involvement—at least in theory. But when it comes to getting down to practicalities too many are unsure where to begin. Here is a handbook which will help in the task of being what Charles Colson called "little platoons of society". Even though this book comes out of the Australian situation, there are many models for action that are replicable in the British context.
John Martin, *Church of England Newspaper*

For Ange

Not Religion
but Love

*Practising
a radical spirituality
of compassion*

Dave Andrews

WIPF & STOCK · Eugene, Oregon

Wipf and Stock Publishers
199 W 8th Ave, Suite 3
Eugene, OR 97401

Not Religion but Love
Practicing a Radical Spirituality of Compassion
By Andrews, Dave and Ringma, Charles
Copyright©1999 by Andrews, Dave
ISBN 13: 978-1-61097-851-4
Publication date 2/1/2012
Previously published by Tafina Press, 1999

Introduction to Dave Andrews for the 2012 Dave Andrews Legacy Series

I KEPT seeing this guy on the shuttle bus - long hair, graying beard, a gentle 60's-70's feel to him. He seemed thoughtful, intense, friendly, and quiet, like he had a lot on his mind, as did I. Even though I saw him nearly every time I boarded the shuttle bus, we didn't speak beyond him smiling and saying, "G'day" and me nodding and saying, "Hey" as we boarded or disembarked.

It was my first time at Greenbelt, a huge festival about faith, art, and justice held every August in the UK. I had always heard great things about the event and so was thrilled when I was invited to speak. I was just as thrilled to get a chance to hear in person some musicians and speakers I had only heard about from a distance, so I went through the program and marked people I wanted to be sure not to miss.

It was near the end of the conference when a friend told me to be sure to catch an Australian fellow named Dave Andrews. "I've never heard of him," I said. "Oh, he's a force of nature," my friend said. "Kind of like Jim Wallis, Tony Campolo, and Mother Teresa rolled up into one." How could I not put a combination like that in one of the last free slots on my schedule?

I arrived at the venue a few minutes late and there he was, the bearded guy from the bus. Thoughtful, intense, and friendly, yes - but *quiet* he was not. He was nearly exploding with passion - passion and compassion, in a voice that ranged from fortissimo to fortississimo to furioso. How could a guy churning with so much hope, love, anger, energy, faith, fury, and curiosity have been so quiet and unassuming on the bus?

He was a force of nature indeed, evoking from his audience laughter, shouts, amens, reverent silence, and even tears before he was done. He spoke of justice, of poverty, of oppression, of solidarity across religious differences, of service, of hope, of celebration, of the way of Jesus.

As I listened, I wanted to kick myself. *This is the most inspiring talk I've heard at this whole festival. Why did I miss all those opportunities to get to know this fellow on the bus? Now the festival is almost over and I've missed my chance!*

Later than evening, I boarded the shuttle bus for the last ride back to my hotel, and there sat Dave and his wife, Ange. I didn't miss my chance this time. I introduced myself and they reciprocated warmly.

I was a largely unknown American author at the time and hardly known at Greenbelt, much less in Australia, so I'm quite certain Dave and Ange had never heard of me. But they couldn't have been kinder, and as we disembarked, he pulled two books from his backpack and told me they were a gift.

The next day when I flew home from Heathrow, I devoured them both on the plane. First, I opened *Not Religion, But Love* and read it through from cover to cover. Then I opened *Christi-anarchy* and couldn't put it down either. When my plane landed, I felt I had been on a spiritual retreat . . . or maybe better said, in a kind of spiritual boot camp!

Things I was thinking but had been afraid to say out loud Dave was saying boldly and confidently. Ideas I was very tentatively considering he had already been living with for years. Complaints and concerns I only shared in highly guarded situations he was publishing from the housetops. Hopes and ideals I didn't dare to express he celebrated without embarrassment.

I think I gave him a copy of one or two of my books as well, and I guess he was favorably impressed enough that we stayed in touch and a friendship developed. I discovered that we were both songwriters as well as writers, that we both had a deep interest in interfaith friendships, that we both had some critics and we both had known the pain of labeling and rejection.

Since then, whatever he has written, I've been sure to read . . . knowing that he speaks to my soul in a way that nobody else does.

We've managed to get together several times since our initial meeting in England, in spite of the fact that we live on opposite sides of the planet. We've spoken together at a few conferences on both hemispheres, and I had the privilege of visiting him in Brisbane. I've seen the beautiful things he has been doing in a particularly interesting and challenging neighborhood there, walking the streets with him, meeting his friends, sensing his love for that place and those people. He's been in my home in the US as well, and we've been conspiring for some other chances to be and work together in the future.

In my speaking across North America, I frequently refer to Dave's work, but until now, his books have been hard to come by. That's why I'm thrilled to introduce this volume to everyone I can in North America.

Yes, you'll find he's one part Tony Campolo, one part Jim Wallis, and one part Mother Teresa, a force of nature, as I was told.

You'll also find he is a serious student of the Bible and a serious theological sage — the kind of reflective activist or thinker-practitioner that we need more of.

In a book like *Christi-anarchy*, he can boldly and provocatively unsettle you and challenge you. Then in a book like *Plan Be*, he can gently and pastorally encourage and inspire you. Like the central inspiration of his life, he is the kind of person to confidently turn over tables in the Temple one minute and then humbly defend a shamed and abused woman from her accusers the next.

You'll see in Dave's writings that he is highly knowledgeable about poverty, ecology, psychology, sociology, politics, and economics . . . not only from an academic standpoint, but also from a grassroots, experiential level. His writing on these subjects grows from what he has done on the ground . . . for example, nurturing a community network that is training young adults to live and serve among the poor, supervising homes for adults who are learning to live with physical and psychiatric disabilities, encouraging small businesses to hire people who others would consider unemployable and developing a non-profit solar energy co-op for local people.

Dave's writings and friendship have meant so much to me. I consider him a friend and mentor. Now I am so happy that people across North America can discover him too.

You'll feel as I did — so grateful that you didn't miss the chance to learn from this one-of-a-kind, un-categorizable, un-containable, wild wonder from Down Under named Dave Andrews.

Brian D. McLaren
author/speaker/activist (brianmclaren.net)

Foreword

Unlike most Christian leaders, Dave Andrews is not a cleric. He is not the pastor of a Christian congregation nor the director of Christian agency. He is not a scholar in a seminary nor a leader at the centre of the church's life. He is a man at the margins.

What makes Dave Andrews so impressive is this – he has chosen to live out his calling in a very different way. Dave is someone who has been captivated by the radical and compassionate Christ. His Jesus is not the person of the stained-glass window, nor of popular religiosity. At an early age, Dave encountered a very different Jesus who later called him, together with his wife Ange, to walk the road of costly discipleship in service to the poor.

This road led him in 1972 to work with travellers on the Asian hippie trail in the Dilaram Houses, extending hospitality and support to the many drug users on the trail. There was nothing ordinary about the young people who came to Dilaram. Many had tripped out on hallucinogenic drugs, indulged in weird religious experiences and were psychologically disturbed. They vomited on the floor, stabbed themselves, and ran naked down the street.

That some of them were healed was both a sign of God's grace and the tenacity of Dave and Ange and their fellow workers. This formative experience led Dave and Ange, together with some Indian friends, to establish Aashiana, an intentional discipleship community in Delhi five years later. Aashiana practised cluster living and simple lifestyle. Out of their life together developed ministries of personal care, social justice, and community development.

Under the auspices of Aashiana, Dave and Ange and their friends set up Sahara to cater for people with personality disorders and drug dependency. Structured as a therapeutic community, Sahara today continues to be a place of refuge and rehabilitation for troubled young people from all over India seeking help, as well as a training program for those wishing to initiate similar ministries.

Out of the Sahara ministry, a community development program, Sharan, was initiated. The link between the two reflects a commitment to holism. Those helped at Sahara were empowered to help others. Renewal is never simply for ourselves. We are also called to serve others. From these tentative beginnings, Sharan today has become one of the largest voluntary organisations working in the slums and resettlement areas of Delhi. Sponsoring educational, health, employment, and other community development programs, Sharan serves thousands of marginalised people who are HIV positive, or have full-blown AIDS, all over India.

Dave had to leave India in 1984 when the government did not renew his visa. That these ministries have not only continued, but have expanded since Dave and Ange's return to Australia, is evidence of their empowering leadership style.

The Andrews' return to Australia meant a new location, but resulted in the pursuit of a similar vision. In this sense, Dave is single-minded and irrepressible. The vision for community, and the care of marginalised people, adapted from their experience in India, not only continued in Australia, but deepened.

The Waiters' Union was born in the inner-city suburb of West End, Brisbane. Here, a network of families and singles living in the local area with Dave and Ange developed a number of programmes working with indigenous people, migrants, refugees, abused women, broken men, and particularly those abandoned by the psychiatric system.

While the Waiters' Union is sometimes wonderfully chaotic, because it is held together by a network of friendships rather than organisational rules and regulations, the vision is clear. It is focused on the life of Jesus of Nazareth, and living out the love and justice that typified his life in the locality. People can join the Waiters by participating in the existing ministries, or by creating new ones. Here, creativity is the order of the day. Their strategy? To work with people rather than for people: sharing good news in the context of friendship, empowering people in a caring setting, connecting people to information and resources, providing people with more choices and a greater control over their lives. While engaging people at the grassroots, they also seek to change unjust structures that disempower the poor and keep them marginalised.

This bare outline of some of the things Dave Andrews has done hardly explains the man, let alone his passion. Labels such as 'activist', 'agitator', or 'prophet' don't help at all. But that Dave is an important leader is a given. That he is not always understood by the church should hardly be surprising.

Dave will always carry a certain mystique. He is a charismatic person both at the speaker's rostrum and face to face. There is an energy that oozes out of him even when he is overworked. My long association with him has convinced me that he is a natural leader with a sharp mind, as well as a very good community worker who has committed himself to empowering the poor.

While inspired by Mahatma Gandhi and Martin Luther King and other leaders, Dave's central impulse comes from his loyalty to Jesus. And this Jesus has kept him in the faith, has kept his heart soft and his imagination strong, and has kept him on the road of servanthood and frequent powerlessness in the face of disappointments.

The fruit of Dave and Ange's life is evident: ministries established, friendships forged, people helped, communities transformed, and workers trained to do likewise. Dave persistently refuses to accept the intolerable and continues to dream that the impossible is possible. In *Christi-Anarchy*, Dave portrays the long history of the project Christendom as the house of authority, with its many attendant abuses of power.

But in the tradition of Vernard Eller, Dave invites us to dwell in the house of freedom, and to fling open all the doors and windows—with welcome, hospitality, and community. In *Not Religion but Love* Dave shows us how we can follow Christ in a way that can set us free to be fully human and fully alive. Read this book. It may well set your heart on fire.

Professor Charles Ringma
Regent College
Vancouver, Canada

Contents

Preface to the Tafina edition

This new edition of *Not Religion but Love* has been specially prepared to accompany *Compassionate Community Work*, the introductory course in Christian community work published by Piquant Press. The text has been completely reset, with revisions for clarity's sake, and a few alterations made to bring the stories and events up to date. There is, for example, a new story about the Sunnybank caravan park in chapter 7. I have added a short description of *Compassionate Community Work* itself at the end of the resources section.

Dave Andrews
April 2006

Preface

When *Christi-Anarchy* was published it met with strong, but mixed, reactions. 'Just when you thought it was safe to navigate the shelves of your local…bookshop,' wrote one reviewer, 'along comes Dave Andrews.' He went on to say that, because *Christi-Anarchy* was such an 'explosive book', it was 'the sort that is bound to kick up debate', but, 'by definition, is a must-read.' Meanwhile a reviewer for the appropriately-named Shoot the Messenger online magazine, was telling anyone who cared to log on that *Christi-anarchy* 'is a truly offensive book—and the author is to be commended!'

Pat Harrison, who teaches at Tabor College in Sydney, said that *Christi-Anarchy* was ' a courageous and provocative study, likely to earn applause from some, and brickbats from others, but certain to challenge and to stimulate serious reflection.' She confesses that 'many of us who teach Church History feel uncomfortable with facile explanations of its dark, demonic side. This book confronts that darkness with a sobering accusation: post-Constantinian Christianity has so perverted the 'Way' that, far from being aberrations, atrocities have become its natural excrescences'. She continues, saying, 'Dave Andrews attacks Christian complacency and calls us back to the non-violent, yet radically subversive 'Way' of Jesus. Christianity's reputation is so besmirched a startling new name (Christi-Anarchy) is proposed for the humble, loving 'Way' of life taught and exemplified by Jesus.' She concludes, 'Those afraid of moving out of their comfort zone are advised not to read this book!'

Among the mixed reactions were wholehearted responses from readers, who were just the kind of people I had in mind when I was writing it. Of particular interest was a letter I received from a young man who had been seeking to live out a Christ-centred anarchistic spirituality for years - without much encouragement.

> Shalom. I'm writing to you after reading your wonderful book *Christi-Anarchy*. The title struck me, as several years ago, I produced a small, self-published pamphlet with the same title. I was involved in the British Anarchist movement, committed to justice and ecology. (Then) I had a Damascus-Road type of experience, and completely independent of any Christian believers, became a born-again Christian overnight. Unfortunately, since that time to this, right up to the present, it has been one big wilderness experience of hurt, rejection, and non-acceptance. I've been rejected by Christians for being an anarchist, and been rejected by anarchists for being a Christian. I've tried to build bridges, but you can never win. At present, I have no spiritual home, and—maybe—I never will. I am interested in God's redemption, not just of individuals, but also of cultures. I would deeply value your comments, and look forward to hearing from you...

This letter raises many issues. There is the age-old issue of how we can find a place that we can call home, or make the place that we live in a little more like home for everyone. There is the issue of how spirituality is actually related to the process of creating a healthy, inclusive human community. There is the issue of how ideology, be it Christian or anarchist, or some combination of both, impacts on the resolution of personal and social problems; and there is the issue of what the life of Jesus of Nazareth, a man who lived over 2000 years ago, has to do with the struggle for justice in our context at the start of the 21st century.

It is precisely these issues that I would like to address in this book.

I would like to express my gratitude to my wife, Ange, my daughters Evonne and Navi, and my son-in-law Marty, who have sought to work out their faith in Christ with me in the context of community.

Both Ange and I are grateful to our parents, Frank and Margaret Andrews and Jim and Athena Bellas, for the role models they provided for us; to our friends in Dilaram and Aashiana who made many of our dreams come true; and the Waiters' Union with whom we live our life in West End.

I am also grateful to David Engwicht, with whom I first wrote the first edition of this book and without whose help it would have been unreadable; and to Roland Lubett of Tafina Press, for re-publishing *Christi-Anarchy*, and *Not Religion but Love*.

Dave Andrews
Brisbane, Australia

Prayers

God help us. With great skill and energy, we have ignored the state of the human heart. With eloquence and wit we have belittled the heart's wisdom. With politics and economics we have denied the heart's needs. With science and technology we have drowned out the voice of the soul. The primitive voice - the innocent voice - the truth.

We cannot hear the heart's truth, and thus we have betrayed and belittled ourselves and pledged madness to our children . . . We have made for ourselves an unhappy society.

It is timely that we give thanks for the lives of all prophets, teachers, healers, and revolutionaries, living and dead, acclaimed or obscure, who have rebelled, worked, and suffered for the cause of love and joy. We also celebrate that part of us, that part of us within ourselves, which has rebelled, worked, and suffered for the cause of love and joy.

God help us to change. To change ourselves and to change our world. To know the need for it. To deal with the pain of it. To feel the joy of it. To undertake the journey without understanding the destination.

That which is Christ-like within us shall be crucified. It shall suffer and be broken. And that which is Christ-like within us shall rise up. It shall love and create.

Excerpts from A Common Prayer *by Michael Leunig*

The Heart of Christ

Christi-Anarchy /kristiæneki/ *n*. Christlike life; lifestyle characterised by the radical nonviolent sacrificial compassion of Jesus the Christ; a way of life distinguished by commitment to love and to justice; working from the bottom up to empower people, particularly the marginalised and disadvantaged, so as to enable them to realise their potential, as men and women, made in the image of God, through self-directed, other-orientated intentional community groups and organisations; from *Christi* – 'Christ', and *anarche* – 'against the powers', as in 'against the principalities and powers'.

1   Radical Spirituality*

We need to begin with the realisation that our world is in trouble; and that religion, which was meant to make things better, has often made things worse. We do not suffer from the lack of religion, but from the lack of love. So if we are to have any hope of survival, we need to find a way to be able to care for ourselves, and for our world, once again. It is my view that a radical spirituality of compassion is not merely our best hope; it is our only hope.

But we may well ask ourselves: how can this generation, which is more troubled than ever before—more disillusioned, more lonely, and more depressed; more anxious, more angry, and more aggressive—how can this generation rediscover the capacity to care enough to save us from destruction? Especially when so often so many of us experience so little care ourselves in the increasingly dysfunctional families, disintegrating communities, and destructive political-economies which shape our lives? And when at every turn we are encouraged to opt, not for care, but for the slick quick-fix kill, which doesn't bother about trying to solve problems, but simply blows them away?

The psychologist, Dan Goleman, says that the question about the survival of humanity is a question that all of us will have to answer in our own hearts. He says that at the heart of the matter is 'empathy'. Empathy is the capacity for us to feel how others feel. It is, he says, in empathising with potential victims—people in danger

---

*   This chapter is a summary of some of the salient ideas introduced in *Christi-Anarchy*. If you have read the book recently and remember the basic gist of its argument, you may want to skip this chapter.

or distress—and feeling how they might feel, that we can be motivated to refrain from harming them, and, hopefully, even perhaps consider helping them.[1] Empathy is the basis of compassion.[2]

The philosopher John Macmurray says that while most of us might be willing to give intellectual assent, in our heads, to the priority for us to rediscover our capacity for empathy, it simply will not happen unless we give some emotional affirmation to that intellectual assent, in our hearts, and make it happen![3] The issue is not so much a conflict between our heads and our hearts, but a conflict that we have in our hearts.[4] In our hearts we know that we cannot live without love. And that love involves an enhanced sensibility: an enhanced appreciation of, and affection for, one another's lives. But in our hearts, we also know that if we develop an enhanced sensibility towards the beautiful yet painful reality of one another's lives, it will inevitably entail great agony as well as great joy. So we vacillate, wanting at the same time to become more loving, and to become anything but more loving.

As we prevaricate, we are tempted to withdraw from sensibility, which involves a greater sensitivity toward the total reality of one another's lives, into sentimentality. This involves more sensitivity to those parts of one another's lives which are less painful (like rumour, innuendo, scandal and trivia), and less sensitivity to those parts of one another's lives that are more painful (like disadvantage, disability, disease and death).[5] Thus we tend to retreat into an unreal world of infotainment, sit-coms, chat-shows, and hot-goss magazines, which give us the illusion of relating to the real world, without actually relating to it at all.

But the only way we can live, is to live in the real world. The only way we can live in the real world, is to love the real world. And the only way we can love the real world, is to overcome our fear of the suffering that love in the real world involves. We must not allow our fear of the suffering to so take over our lives that we put all our efforts into building up our defences against the world, and so alienate ourselves from the very reality to which we need to relate. We need to find a faith that can help us overcome our fear of suffering, so that we can embrace the world as it is, love it, warts and all, and live our lives, with friend and foe alike, to the full.[6] The only way I know of that any of us can do that, is by following the way of Christ.[7]

Now having said that, in case any of you have an apoplectic fit, let me say very clearly, that for me, Christ is not synonymous with Christianity. They are not one and the same. In fact the way advocated by Christ is in many cases a total contradiction of the way that is advocated by Christianity. In many cases, Christianity has simply co-opted Christ. It has taken his love, and turned it into a religion. It bears his name, but betrays his legacy of relentless tenderness. Christianity may stand for a Christ-ian ideology. But Christ himself stands with us against all ideology —particularly any Christ-ian ideology—that people might try to impose on us. He calls us not to a Christ-ian ideology, but to a Christ-like sensibility.

Mahatma Gandhi, the great Hindu sage, suggested that if Christ could only be unchained from the shackles of Christianity, he could become 'The Way', not just for Christians, but for the whole world. 'The gentle figure of Christ—so patient, so kind, so loving, so full of forgiveness that he taught his followers not to retaliate when struck, but to turn the other cheek—was a beautiful example, I thought, of the perfect person.'[8] Christ was 'an embodiment of sacrifice', and 'a factor in the composition of my underlying faith in non-violence, which rules all my actions.'[9] Actually, Gandhi said, 'I refuse to believe that there exists a person who has not made use of his example, even though he or she may have done so without realising it'. He went on to say that 'the lives of all have, in some greater or lesser degree, been changed by his presence. And because Jesus has the significance, and transcendency to which I have alluded, I believe he belongs not to Christianity, but to the entire world; to all people, it matters little what faith they profess.'[10] 'Leave Christians alone for the moment', he concluded, 'I shall say to the Hindus that your lives will be incomplete unless you reverently study ... Jesus.'[11] 'Jesus did not preach a new religion, but a new life': 'a whole life' regulated by 'the eternal law of love.'[12]

I believe, like Gandhi, that Christ is the archetype of compassion, the original model of radical nonviolent sacrificial love, that humanity desperately needs to turn to if we are to find a way to save ourselves from the cycles of violence that will otherwise destroy us.[13] A recent survey in *Psychology Today* showed that Gandhi and I are not alone in that belief. Apparently, even more than 2000 years after he lived and died in obscurity in Palestine, it is to Jesus of Nazareth that most of us who know anything about him still feel we need to turn, if we are ever really going to learn anything about radical, nonviolent, sacrificial love.[14] As the famous analytical psychiatrist, Carl Jung, once said:

One of the most shining examples that history has preserved for us is the life of Christ. Obeying the inner call of his vocation, Jesus voluntarily exposed himself to the assaults of imperial madness that filled everyone, conqueror, and conquered alike. In this way he recognised the nature of the psyche which had plunged the whole world into misery. Far from allowing himself to be suppressed by this psychic onslaught, he consciously assimilated it. Thus was a world-conquering Roman Empire transformed into the universal Kingdom of

God. His religion of love was the exact psychological counterpoint to the politics of power. Jesus pointed humanity [to] the truth that where force rules there is no love, and where love reigns force does not count. [15]

I call this radical spirituality of compassion—'where love reigns' and 'force does not count'—not Christianity, but Christi-Anarchy. Christi-Anarchy is not a Christian ideology, or an anarchist ideology, or a Christian-anarchist ideology. Christi-Anarchy is not an ideology at all. If anything, Christi-Anarchy is anti-ideology. For Christi-Anarchy is nothing more or less than a Christ-like sensibility.

Christi-Anarchy derives its name from *Christi*: 'Christ', and *anarche*: 'against the powers'; as Christ himself was against 'the powers'. Any Christ-like sensibility will always struggle against the powers that conspire against ordinary people realising their potential. It is a Christ-like life: a lifestyle that is characterised by the radical, nonviolent, sacrificial compassion of Jesus the Christ. A way of life distinguished by commitment to love and to justice, working from the bottom up to empower people, particularly the marginalised and disadvantaged; so as to enable them to realise their potential, as men and women made in the image of God, through self-directed, other-orientated intentional community groups and organisations.

Christ himself is our example, and his spirit serves as the inspiration for the simple, practical, compassionate path he wants us to take, regardless of the difficulties we may encounter along the way. His expectation is not that we slavishly copy him, but that we voluntarily make the same kind of choices that he made, and that he encouraged his disciples to make—to accept life, to respect life, and to empower people to live life to the full.

Christ calls us to know God, the source of all life, more fully, and to cultivate the disciplines that will help us develop a relationship to God in the midst of our ordinary everyday lives. He calls us to live in sympathy with the heart of God, sustaining ourselves, supporting one another, and serving those around about us, in an increasingly steadfast, faithful, and life-affirming manner.

Christ calls us to be aware of ourselves, and the gift of life, that each of us can bring to the community. He calls us to recognise not only the reality of our weaknesses, but also the reality of our strengths, and our responsibility to grow individually as people, in our capacity for self-care, self-control, and self-sacrifice, for the sake of the community.

Christ calls us to be aware of one another, and the gift of life that everyone else can bring to the community. He calls us to acknowledge not only the reality of our brokenness, but also the potential for wholeness in our relationships, and our responsibility to grow collectively as people, in our capacity to speak truthfully, listen attentively, and work co-operatively, for the sake of the community.

Christ calls us, over and over again, particularly to remember those people in the community who are forgotten, rejected, neglected and ignored. He calls us to affirm our commitment to the welfare of the whole of the human family, and to make ourselves available to brothers and sisters who are marginalised, in their ongoing struggle for love and justice.

Christ knows we disagree about many things, but he wants us to agree at least on one thing: the need for us to join together to develop communities in our localities that reflect his compassion by being more devoted, more inclusive, and more nonviolent.[16]

Ideas for meditation, discussion, and action

Recall: What is Christi-Anarchy?

Reflect: Why is the example of Christ so important?

Relate: How do we relate to the example of Christ ourselves?

2 Revolutionary Sympathy

One balmy Sabbath, Jesus visited the Synagogue in Nazareth and was asked to take the scripture reading. Turning to a passage from the book of the Prophet Isaiah he read: 'The Spirit of God has got hold of me, and is urging me to take on a special task; to share good news with the poor; free the prisoners; help the handicapped; and smash the shackles of the oppressed.'

Luke 4:18–19

Jesus made this statement his manifesto, the mandate for his own mission in life. It reflected his understanding that everything that he wanted to do emerged from his engagement with the Spirit of God. To Jesus, God was love. He believed that whoever knew God knew love, but whoever did not know love did not know God. For God was love.

To Jesus, the Spirit of God was the Spirit of love. For him to open himself to God's Spirit meant opening himself to God's passion. In point of fact, Jesus claimed that God's passion had so penetrated his being, that it set every fibre of his being on fire, with a burning desire for love and for justice that would not be denied. Jesus was in truth a man possessed.

There was never a time when Jesus was so pre-occupied that there was no space for the Spirit in his life. He continually made time to create the space in his life to respond to the prompting of the Spirit. Even in the midst of a pressing schedule, Jesus would take time out to go into the mountains to pray, like a son laying his head on his Father's heart to listen to his heartbeat. After these sessions in solitude he would say, 'I and my Father are one.' The impetus that motivated God, motivated Jesus; they were one and the same.

The Spirit of God set the agenda for Jesus. It inspired the creative, yet controversial actions that he took, and gave him courage to carry them through, regardless of the consequences. According to Jesus, the concern of the Spirit was for the plight of the 'poor'—victims of cruel, systemic injustice, and the predicament of the 'prisoners' and the 'handicapped'—locked out of all meaningful participation in society by rigid bars of steel and stigma. The concern of the Spirit was particularly for people in whom all hope had been crushed, who felt consigned to long days, and even longer nights, of quiet desperation.

According to Jesus, the commitment of the Spirit was to motivate someone to share the good news with the 'forgotten': that they had not been forgotten but had always been remembered—at least by God! The commitment of the Spirit was to motivate someone to embody this good news to the forgotten; by being prepared to struggle in solidarity with them, for release from all the forces that would debilitate them in their abandoned and forgotten state; and by being determined to set them free to realise their potential—to be fully human and fully alive, and fully 're-membered members' of the human community.

Jesus took the Spirit of God to heart. He made the concerns and commitment of the Spirit his own. He became a person who was forgetful of himself, yet lived in constant remembrance of those in the community who were in distress. He used all of his time, his energy and his resources to address their distress. He struggled with them for their liberty. He did not view his role in the community as a religious or a secular carer. To him it was essentially a spiritual struggle for the total liberation of all the people in the community.

Being a devotee of Jesus is not a matter of subscribing to a certain set of dogmas, and getting others to obey rules and regulations. The essence of being a devotee of Jesus is to live in sympathy with God as Jesus did, feeling the throb of God's heartbeat, and teaching our hearts to learn to beat in sync with the love that sustains the universe. It means developing our capacity to intuitively sense what causes love pleasure, and what causes love pain, and doing everything we can to enhance the pleasure, and to diminish the pain.

According to Jesus, God is overjoyed whenever love becomes reality in our lives, and when we seek to do justice to one another, in spirit and in truth. According to Jesus, God is agonised whenever we forget to love one another, and neglect our responsibility to do justice to one another. Whenever we share our food with the hungry, Jesus says, God smiles with pure delight. But whenever we plunge the knife of oppression into the heart of the poor, Jesus tells us that God himself is actually struck a mortal blow.

It was our parents who taught my wife Ange and me, as kids, to live in sympathy with God, as Jesus did; and to do everything we could to pay homage to God by honouring the people we met, as people made in the image of God, regardless of colour, culture, or religion.

My mother and father, Margaret and Frank Andrews, not only took people into their hearts, but also into their home. Home was always open for those in distress. People going through difficult times would stay for a day, a year, or as long as they needed. As a young impressionable boy I can remember the excitement that some of those people brought to our house. A cat burglar, who had just got out of jail, showed us how easy it was to break into our house. My parents never bothered locking the house after that!

Not all these encounters were exciting. Some were actually pretty scary for a kid like me with a vivid imagination. Having a man who had stabbed someone to death, sleeping in the same house as me, made for some very restless nights and some very graphic nightmares! But my parents taught me to relate to these people as people, not as a subhuman species with tags like 'robbers' and 'murderers'—and as people, they got respect.

Ange's parents, James and Athena Bellas, operated the Star Milk Bar in downtown Brisbane. It was famous for its food and drinks. People would come from all over town for a fresh salad sandwich and a mango milk shake. Very early every morning, my father-in-law would open up the café. When he did, it seemed like all the hobos around town would emerge from the hiding places they had huddled in during the night, and make their way to the café. My father-in-law would welcome them in, sit them down, serve them tea and toast, and chat with them about the night they'd had and the day ahead.

If anyone needed a job, my father-in-law would leave his brothers in charge of the café and go job-hunting with them. If they got in trouble with the police, he would visit them in prison. He regularly visited those who fell sick and wound up in hospital. When anyone friendless died, my father-in-law would make sure he went to their funeral, so that no-one, no matter how friendless, would be buried without a friend. Often he'd be the only one there.

Ange's dad would invite folk home to share a meal with the family, even though Ange's mum had eight children of her own to feed. If anything, meals at the Bellas' house were even more famous than the milkshakes at the Star Milk Bar, so there was never a shortage of people willing to take up the invite—or just invite themselves! Ange grew up in a large family, which was always being enlarged to make room for one more; her parents taught her the importance of being family to those who had no family. In so doing they introduced Ange to the Greek practice of *symbetheri*, profound reciprocal regard for family; but at the same time, they totally revolutionised the traditional practice of *symbetheri* to include people like the Turks, their traditional enemies.

Frank and Margaret Andrews, and James and Athena Bellas, have been shining examples of those who are not preoccupied with themselves. As they made time and space for God, they made time and space for the people God cares for so passionately. So Ange and I have, not slavishly, but unashamedly tried to copy our parents, and tried to set a similar example for our children to the one they set for us: of divinely-inspired, profoundly human care.

In 1973 we set up some communities in India that we called *Dilaram*, or Houses of the Peaceful Heart, to cater for weary travellers, trekking up and down the Asian hippie trail in search of enlightenment, or a cheap hallucinogenic substitute. So it was, in the context of living in a *Dilaram* community, working with disillusioned heroin addicts who never found nirvana, except the one at the end of a needle, that our elder daughter Evonne learned her first few lessons about helping people with life-controlling problems.

In 1975 we left *Dilaram*, which was working mainly with foreigners, to set up *Aashiana* to work solely with local drug addicts. *Aashiana* literally meant 'nest', and we hoped it would be a nest where 'wounded birds' could mend their broken wings and learn to fly freely again. We helped people on the condition that they would help others. So naturally, out of *Sahara*, the residential rehabilitation community, emerged *Sharan*, an unusual, innovative, community development organisation, staffed mainly by ex-drug addicts, who were learning to use their understanding of despair to serve communities who knew nothing but despair.

So it was, in the context of the *Aashiana* community, rehabilitating addicts and rebuilding slums, that our younger adopted daughter, Navi, learned her first few lessons about helping people overcome life-controlling problems that otherwise would end in debilitating despair.

In 1985 we returned to Australia, and set up an intentional community network, that we call 'The Waiters' Union', in an inner-city suburb of Brisbane, our home town. Ange's mum and dad live just up the road from us. So we have come full circle, back to where we started from. We still draw reassurance from the example of Ange's parents' involvement in the locality. And we still try to set a similar example for our children, of divinely-inspired, profoundly human care, for the people in the community.

We live in a joint household on one of the main streets of West End. Until recently, Evonne and her husband Marty lived in a house with Navi, their childhood friend Olivia and a couple of others who came and went. They set up the household themselves as a place devoted to developing an everyday spirituality, that willingly puts itself at the disposal of the young people who come looking for help. It has been awesome for Ange and me to see Evonne and Marty and Navi and Olivia living simply, with a common purse, growing their own fruit and vegetables, and sharing their meagre meals generously with the seemingly endless line of unexpected guests that turn up at their place day and night. Not long ago Olivia moved to Adelaide, and Evonne and Marty and Navi invited Ange and me to move in with them.

We gladly accepted their invitation and settled on a house in Hardgrave Road, right in the heart of West End. It is a lovely big old wooden Queensland-style house next to a bus stop, right across the road from half-a-dozen Chinese, Thai, Vietnamese, Indian, Tibetan, and Nepalese restaurants, and the Checocho which is well-known and well-loved for its top-quality, gentle hospitality. If you ever come looking for us, and can't find us at home, pop across the road. Chances are we'll either be eating butter chicken and naan or mango and sticky rice at one of the restaurants, drinking cups of coffee with Evonne and Navi's friends, or discussing co-op business with Marty at Checochos. When we're home, Ange and I live upstairs with Navi and our cat Azmi; Marty and Evonne live downstairs with their kids Lila and Kaedin, their dog Rasta, and the three guests who are staying with them at the moment. Being at the heart of West End has given us the opportunity to increase our involvement in the lives of the people round about us.

It has been one of the greatest joys of our lives to see Evonne and Navi individuate themselves, without isolating themselves from us or our world in the process. As an extended family, we are continuing to extend ourselves, as *symbetheri,* to those in the community who have no family at all. It isn't easy. In fact, sometimes it's quite hard. It always has been. It always will be. Caring, no matter how divinely inspired, is always a profoundly painful human activity. But in a society that pressures people relentlessly to move from dependence to independence, rather than towards the interdependence that our world so desperately needs, God knows it is a miracle that it ever happens at all.

Ideas for meditation, discussion, and action

Recall: What, if any, is our experience of Christ?

Reflect: How do we think Christ feels about people?

Relate: How can we become more sympathetic towards others?

3 Liberating Sensibility

Wherever Jesus went he was surrounded by people. People were so persistent in clamouring for his attention that Jesus often went days without a moment to himself. People were instinctively repulsed by the arrogant judgmentalism of the Pharisees, his self-righteous co-religionists; but they intuitively revelled in the gracious, non-judgmental manner of Jesus, this amazingly loving man, who seemed to have such a liberated and liberating sensibility.

Jesus was once invited to a meal at the home of a Pharisee by the name of Simon.

Simon paced uneasily up and down the verandah, waiting for the first guests to arrive at his dinner party. This was his big opportunity to impress. After all, it wasn't just anybody who could promise a dinner party with the famous Jesus from Nazareth as the guest of honour.

The dinner got off to a great start. Jesus seemed to be the perfect guest for a dinner party. He had the knack of putting people around him at ease. He soon had the other guests engrossed in his homespun yarns, laughing at his one-liners and applauding his punch-lines.

As the entrée dishes were being collected by the servants, Simon listened to the animated chatter that filled the room, and inwardly smiled. His guests were enjoying themselves.

But suddenly the hilarity died. Wondering what on earth could have gone wrong, Simon looked up, and, to his amazement, standing in the doorway was the local prostitute.

Her perfume filled the room and hung like an unanswered question in the night air. Nervously the dignitaries turned to their meal in silence. Her very presence inflamed privately-hidden feelings of shame, and fired publicly-constructed displays of scorn.

Slowly she made her way to the head of the table where the guest of honour reclined. She stood beside him, waiting hesitantly, unsure as to what to do next. Sensing her presence, Jesus turned his head towards her and looked at her. She had looked into the eyes of many men, and only ever seen eyes filled with lust, mingled with pity or contempt. But as she looked into the eyes of this man, she saw his eyes filled with love—not lust, love: a kind of love she had never come across before; a love that touched her hidden wounds with tenderness, recognised her weakness but did not condemn her, and revealed a strength of character in her that she never knew she had.

Embraced so gently by his gaze, the prostitute burst into tears, sobbing deeply. Hot tears streamed through her heavy make-up, ran down her face, and fell on the feet of Jesus. Oblivious to the embarrassment of the other guests, the prostitute unwrapped her hair, took strands of hair in her hands, and, with the tresses, began to wipe the tears from Jesus' feet.

What happened next was a scene that none of the guests—or their host—would ever forget. For men to speak to women in public was forbidden. For men and women to touch in public was completely taboo. Yet, as if in total privacy, the prostitute publicly enacted a strange ritual of love for Jesus. Taking an expensive jar of perfumed cream, she massaged it into the feet that she had already washed with her tears and wiped with her hair.

As Simon the Pharisee looked on, Jesus took the prostitute by the hand, lifted her to her feet and said, 'Thank you for showing your love for me so beautifully. I love you just as you are—even if others don't. Go in peace.'
Luke 7:36-50

What was it about this man that made this woman feel so comfortable in his presence that she could enter a stranger's house uninvited, deliberately break social taboos before a hostile crowd, and outwardly display her inner feelings for him in such a passionate fashion?

I think there was an irresistible attraction to Jesus, because like the prostitute, people found in him a complete and total acceptance, unconditional and non-condemnatory. An acceptance that was neither patronising nor manipulative, but characterised by a profound respect that powerfully transformed their lack of self-esteem into courageous self-respect.

Through the culture of sensibility that he cultivated in his relationships with people, regardless of their status, Jesus was able to create a refuge where outcasts felt safe to drop their pretence, discard their masks, stop playing games and start becoming their real selves. Those who shared their secrets with Jesus found he did not point the finger at their faults, but was more than willing to lend them a hand to deal with their failure, and their fear of failure. Through his liberated and liberating sensibility, Jesus created a liberated and liberating space for people to be free to explore their potential, to be the very best that they could be.

The effect that extending care to one another can actually have is amazing. I vividly remember the day Brenda turned up at our house. She was drugged out of her mind. She visited every day for a while, but then suddenly stopped. Ange went with Brenda's brother, who was staying with us, to find out how she was. When they arrived, Brenda was sitting on the roof of her house. She had stolen her mother's jewellery to sell in exchange for some drugs, had phoned her dealer, and was waiting for the delivery—for some strange reason, sitting on the roof. After being coaxed down from the roof, Brenda ran to the bathroom, locked the door and slit her wrists. Brenda's brother broke the door down, and Ange was able to get into the bathroom, bandage her wrists, and staunch the bleeding.

Brenda was obviously a very distraught person, who was going to need far more than a pep talk to help her come to terms with, and overcome, her distress. Ange decided to bring Brenda home to stay with us, where she felt she could care for her more adequately. So for the next five months Ange spent all day every day by Brenda's side; and slowly, but surely, the two of them became good friends. In the context of the affirmation and affection that their friendship afforded, Brenda was able rediscover the confidence she needed to face the woman she saw in the mirror when she got up in the morning, and to begin to deal with her issues—not only the surface issues, like drugs, but also the deep issues that caused her pain, and were the reason she took drugs to begin with.

Ange helped Brenda start her own small business making handmade stationery. She became a volunteer in an organisation working with drug addicts, married one of the co-ordinators, and, with her husband, ended up running a rehabilitation programme.

However caring is not always so simple or straightforward. Sometimes it can be quite complicated and difficult, even a bit forbidding, as Jesus himself discovered when the prostitute embraced him in public. Ange and I had a very similar experience ourselves.

Anne had a notorious sexual history, and everyone around town seemed to know the score in detail. We were new in town, but it didn't take us very long to learn the reason that everyone was so well informed about Anne's love life. When Anne would come to visit us, as often as not, she would grab any available male that she met in our house as a prop for an impromptu carnal display and begin kissing him profusely, and passionately, in front of everyone. Then when the star of the show had everyone's attention, she would turn to her audience and tell them about her sexual adventures in salacious detail.

Both Ange and I wanted to extend acceptance to Anne, but we weren't sure how to do it in a way that would not encourage her to continue acting in the extravagantly lascivious style that made her an easy mark at local parties. We spent quite a bit of time talking about it, until we came up with a plan that we thought would give Anne the attention she needed, without having to flaunt herself to get it. The plan was simple. Any time Anne felt the need to kiss anyone, she could kiss Ange, not the nearest available male. And any time Anne felt the need to talk about sex, she could talk to Ange, not the crowd in our lounge room.

When we told Anne about the plan she was rapt. So, from then, on every time Anne felt the urge to kiss someone, she would go to Ange and cover her with kisses. At least once a day, every day for the next six months, Ange would find herself lost in a frenzy of kissing. During this time, we encouraged Anne to relate to people, in public, more intimately, but less sexually; and to discuss her sexual issues with Ange in private. We did not condemn Anne over her sexual behaviour. Instead we communicated her value as a person. And Anne began to feel the joy of being loved, not for her utilitarian value as a sex object, but for her intrinsic value as a human being.

The culture of respect that we created, provided a context in which Anne could discover herself as a person: both the person she was, and the person she desperately wanted to be—a person who could love and be loved with dignity as a human being, not a sex object. So Anne began the long slow process of transformation. As yet the transformation is neither permanent nor complete. But Anne, who was previously unemployable, has had a job as a well-regarded administrative assistant in a company for a number of years. And there is an unmistakable air of dignity about her that once was only a dream.

The problems associated with extending authentic care aren't always so easily resolved. Some who want to care for others intimately, get involved sexually with the people they are helping, and so end up exploiting the people they started out trying to help. Others, who are scared of colluding with—let alone indulging in— any inappropriate sexual behaviour, keep themselves so separate from the people they are trying to help, that they are often of no help to anyone at all. It seems to me, we would do a lot better if we found a way of caring for others that more faithfully reflected the liberating sensibility of Christ.

John Hughes, a friend of mine who is a local doctor, once told me about his efforts to find a way of caring for two of his patients, both prostitutes, that reflected the sensibility of Christ more faithfully. We'll call them Jenny and Jane.

Jenny moved to Brisbane when her marriage broke up. She arrived at John's medical clinic and John arranged some emergency assistance for Jenny and her family. But Jenny became frustrated with living on welfare, and told John that she wanted to take up a job she had been offered as a sex worker with a local 'escort agency', in order to get more money to support her family. Jenny asked John if he would respect her choice to be a sex worker and support her in her choice of work, by keeping her free from STDs, sexually transmitted diseases. This request presented John with a very difficult ethical dilemma. On the one hand, as a Christian, John was committed to sharing in Jenny's struggle to regain the dignity of choice in her life; but on the other hand, as a Christian, John was committed to advocating healthy lifestyle choices, which as far as he was concerned, did *not* include prostitution!

John felt that the best thing he could do for Jenny was to try to encourage her to change her mind. So John spent the next hour in his surgery begging Jenny to consider a range of other alternatives. But he failed to persuade her. Jenny's argument was that she would be providing a necessary service to the community, and that John, as her doctor, should support her in providing that service as safely as possible. John said he wanted to help her, but couldn't condone prostitution. So Jenny left. And John has never seen her again.

Jane presented herself at John's medical clinic with pelvic pain and vaginal discharge. Jane told John that she was a 'working girl', and she needed him, as her doctor, to help her to cope with the occupational hazards of her work, like the STD she had presented with. With Jane, John faced the same ethical dilemma that had confronted him with Jenny. He didn't know what to do with Jane; but he knew he didn't want to do as he had done with Jenny. Since the day she had left his surgery, John had been troubled by regret over his response to Jenny. With Jane walking into his office the way she did, John felt he was being given a chance to redeem himself by caring for a prostitute like Jenny, but more appropriately. He decided that this time round, he would not take the moral high ground, as a Christian; instead, he would climb down from his moral high horse, join his patient at her point of pain, and simply do all he could to help her, as Christ would.

So John told Jane that he would respect her choice of work and he would support her, by keeping her free from STDs, as she had requested him to do; but he wanted to remain in dialogue with her about her work, and the impact that her work had upon her as a person. He assured her that he would be there for her, whatever she decided to do; and that he would be there for her, particularly, if those choices got her into trouble.

Weeks went by. John saw Jane a number of times about a range of medical issues. And whenever they met they talked. Gradually John got to hear more and more of Jane's story. In many ways it was just like Jenny's. Like Jenny, Jane's marriage had broken up, and she had two kids to support. Like Jenny, Jane felt 'working' was better than welfare. And like Jenny, she said she was providing an essential service to the community.

But Jane was not Jenny. Her story was her own. And as he listened, Jane told John about her struggle to keep 'working', and looking after her children, at the same time; she knew her lifestyle was unsettling them, so she sent the kids to be with their father for a while; but he was preventing her from having access to them, because of her profession. Her life was starting to come unstuck, but she was tough, and she was determined to tough it out.

One day Jane turned up and collapsed into a chair across from John. 'My dad is dead', she said. Jane had had a love-hate relationship with her alcoholic father..On one level she was glad he was dead. But on another level she was sad about his death. John tried to enter into her sense of loss, and share her feeling of grief as best he could. Jane responded to the support by bursting into tears, crying; 'I am so useless. I couldn't relate to my dad. I can't care for my own kids. I'm fucked!' John wasn't sure what to say. Then, very deliberately, John leaned towards Jane, and said; 'You're fucked. I'm fucked. But Christ came to help fucked-up people like you and me.' Jane could scarcely believe her ears. Here was John, the straightlaced Christian medical practitioner—whom she had never heard swear—speaking hope to her in her own words. John says he was almost as surprised as Jane. But after they got over the shock, they talked for a long while together, about the possibilities of putting the pieces of her life back together again. On the way out, Jane burst into tears again, and John gave her a big hug, in front of all the astonished patients in the waiting room.

John saw Jane a few weeks later. After her dad's funeral she had gone to stay with her mum in a country town. While she was there she decided to quit her work, reclaim her kids, move back home with her family, and start her life all over again. Which is what she did. Upon reflection, John says, 'Christ's love had worked a miracle in both our lives.' By giving Jane a chance, John had another chance to become more human himself.

Ideas for meditation, discussion, and action

Recall: Remember a time when you met someone on the periphery of society. How did you actually react to them at the time?

Reflect: How did Christ relate to people on the periphery?

Relate: How do we respond to the way Christ related to people on the periphery?

4 Practical Compassion

It is one thing to be interested in people; it is quite another actually to get involved. Relating to others comes naturally to some people, but not to all of us—certainly not to me. I'm more an 'ideas' person than a 'people' person. I'm into people because I think it's a good idea. But because I'm an ideas person, rather than a people person, I still find it difficult to get involved with people, even if it is a good idea, in a manner that is truly compassionate.

Many are particularly uncomfortable around people on the fringe of society. They represent needs we cannot meet—questions we cannot answer. They make us feel quite inadequate. We think we don't have the qualifications to deal with them. So when we think of working with them, we think of either training as an expert, or employing one. The logic is obvious, the rationale is clear: people need professional help. We simply don't have the expertise ourselves to be involved. Helping others is a job that is better left for the experts.

But Jesus had little time for experts. Jesus never trained in a 'rabbinic' school, the tertiary college of the day; nor was Jesus ever ordained as a 'rabbi' or a qualified teacher. He wasn't a doctor or a lawyer. He wasn't even a counsellor. He was a carpenter, just one of the gang. Not only did he not have professional welfare expertise, he constantly attacked the arrogant authority that the experts ascribed to themselves—not because he despised the expertise of the experts, but because he despised the way that many were using their expertise as a means of exploiting the very people they were supposed to be helping.

As far as I'm concerned it is still pretty much the same today. Many welfare organisations, religious and secular, are fronts for exploitation of the poor. In fact, such organisations have a vested interest in keeping poor people poor, because if the people are dependent on the services of an organisation for their survival, then the organisation has to survive in order to ensure their survival; and there's no better argument for the continued funding of a welfare organisation than the welfare of its clients. If you don't believe me, let me ask you a question: when was the last time you heard of a welfare organisation closing its doors because it had so effectively empowered those it sought to help that the organisation became redundant? No wonder Jesus rejected welfare as the way of liberating the oppressed!

Jesus did not leave the task of helping people to the experts. He simply helped them help themselves. And the amazing thing about his way of helping people was, that when ordinary, uneducated, unqualified, and apparently totally inept people, followed this approach, they often had a far more dramatic effect on helping people in a community realise their potential than a whole army of experts could ever hope to have achieved.

The approach advocated by Christ was one of practical compassion. Paul unpacks the implications of Christ's example of practical compassion for us when he writes:

> Each of you should not look to your own interests, but also to the interests of others. You should have exactly the same attitude as Christ Jesus had:
>
> For he who had always been God by nature, did not cling to his prerogatives as God's equal, but he stripped himself of all privilege, emptied himself, and made himself nothing, in order to be born by nature as a mortal. And, having become a

human being, he humbled himself, living the life of a slave, a life of utter obedience, even unto death. And the death he died, on the cross, was the death of a common criminal.
Philippians 2:6-8

Paul points out that, as the story goes, Christ moved in alongside us, as one of us. He did not try to be different. He lived the same life that other people lived, experiencing the same hassles and the same hardships as everybody else. Christ wasn't full of himself. But, emptying himself, he immersed himself in the lives of others, allowing their concerns to fill his consciousness. In the midst of their common struggle, Christ made himself available to the people as their servant, seeking in all he said and did, to set them free to live their lives to the full. When it came to the crunch, Christ did not cut and run. He was prepared to pay the price for his commitment to people—in blood, sweat, and tears.

Paul says practising compassion means taking the approach Christ took ourselves. It is not something we can do vicariously through others. It is something we must do ourselves. There is a role for organisations: they may provide a useful framework for the work we want to do in the community. There is also a role for professionals: they may provide extra insight, knowledge, and skill that is useful for increasing the effectiveness of the work we want to do. But there is simply no substitute for our face-to-face, hands-on, grass-roots involvement. If we're going to get involved like Christ did, we've got to get our hands dirty too.

We must be willing to set aside our concerns for security and status. We must be willing to forgo the comforts that privilege and position bring, in order to meet people, many of whom who are profoundly disadvantaged and distressed, on their territory and on their terms. We must try, not to be different from the people around us, but to discover the similarities we share in the humanity that runs as blood through our veins. We all get sick. We all get tired. We all grow old. But we all want to love and be loved. And we all want to live life to the full before we die. We can share these common struggles with our brothers and sisters in the human community— even if our economics, politics, culture, and religion are poles apart.

We must empty ourselves of our preoccupation with our own thoughts and feelings, so that we can immerse ourselves in the lives of others, and allow their joy and their anguish to fill our lives. We must enter into people's struggles with them, and, in the context of that struggle, serve them as a servant: not like a public servant, but like a personal servant. Our relationships with people should be marked by an uncommon quality of care: a quality of life that reflects the love of Christ, who came not to be served, but to serve, and to give his life as the price he was willing to pay to bring life to people in the community.

If we are to have any hope of bringing life to people in *our* community, we too must be willing to pay the price, by dying to ourselves in the midst of the inevitable frustrations, tensions, difficulties and conflicts that work in the community always entails. There is no easy option. If there were, Christ would have taken it. He was a messiah, not a masochist. Christ took the hard path because it was the only path that he could take that would lead to the practice of compassion. For those of us who would follow in his footsteps, there is no other way than to open our heart and risk the heartache, and the heartbreak, of real involvement in people's lives. Compassion comes from *com* meaning 'with', and *passion* meaning 'suffering'; so to practise compassion means 'being willing to suffer with others' as Christ did.

For many of us, this may seem like an unrealistic ideal, achievable only by saints, and not by mere mortals like you and me. Well it is certainly an ideal, but it's not unrealistic. I have met many less-than-perfect individuals who live out this ideal in a less-than-perfect world. Freda is one such woman. Freda is a medical practitioner. She could earn a big income, drive a big car, live in a big house, and enjoy the kudos of being a doctor. But she doesn't. She has rejected the prestige that comes with being a doctor. Most people don't even know she is a doctor; they just relate to her as Freda. Freda rides a bike around the neighbourhood and greets strangers in the street. She is not full of herself and her own opinions. She gives other people space to be themselves and have their say.

Freda works for Aboriginal Health, but not as a medical expert who commutes from a middle-class suburb. Freda lives where they live, and fights the battles they fight. She takes to the streets with them to protest at injustice and cops the same abuse they get. She gives most of her substantial income away and lives on a meagre allowance so she can identify more closely with those she seeks to help. Freda shows the difference between service and servanthood. Acts of service are those acts we decide to do in our efforts to help others. Acts of servanthood are those acts others decide they would like us to do for them. Freda has felt the heartbeat of God for her community and responded by giving herself as a servant to those she seeks to help. Freda is having a quiet but significant impact on her community.

My daughters Evonne and Navi are also having a significant impact on their community, simply by living in the neighbourhood, relating to their neighbours, and identifying with some of our most distressed and disadvantaged neighbours. Freda's story shows that anybody—even a doctor—can be compassionate. Evonne and Navi's story shows we don't have to be a doctor in order to be able to practise compassion.

Some of our most marginalised neighbours are people who have been de-institutionalised, put out of psychiatric hospitals in the hope that, by being placed in a community, rather than in an institution, their lives will be normalised. However, most of the people being placed in our community are not placed with families. After all, very few families—even their own—would welcome them home. So they are being placed in hostels.

When we started visiting the hostels, it became painfully obvious that the vast majority of the hostel residents had no significant reciprocal relationships with people living outside—other than people like case workers, who were paid to relate to them. It was a state of affairs that we felt was not very healthy for anyone's sense of self-esteem. So Evonne, then Navi, decided they would try to befriend a few people in a local hostel. Evonne decided she would try to get alongside a woman whom I shall refer to as Rita. Now Rita was pretty much completely friendless. And to be frank, one of the major reasons that Rita had no friends, was that no one who knew her well, really wanted to be her friend! Rita was very difficult to relate to. I must confess that I've occasionally described her, in jest, as 'the grumpiest woman in the world'; and no one who knew her—not even Evonne, who loved her dearly—ever said that my description of her was unfair.

I first met Rita when she came up behind me unexpectedly, and pushed me off the chair I was sitting on. I looked up, and there was a very angry chubby seventy-year-old woman staring down at me, snarling, 'That's my chair, mister!' I looked around, saw the room had sixty to seventy empty chairs scattered round it, and suggested that surely she could have taken another seat if she wanted one, as the one I had been sitting on was exactly the same as all the others. But she just said 'That's my chair, mister! Get another one yourself!'

In my next encounter with her, Rita continued her policy of driving right over the top of me like a heavy laden truck rolling over a speed bump. One night I remember serving tea and biscuits when I saw Rita approaching the counter at full speed. I gave her a cup of tea, and was in the middle of telling her only to take one biscuit, till everyone had a chance to have one, when she thrust both her mitts into the biscuit tin, grabbed as many biscuits as she could hold in her chubby fists, and stuffed half a tin of biscuits in her mouth, all at once!

I wasn't the only one who found Rita difficult to relate to. When I took people from her hostel out on picnics, I noticed that no one would want to sit next to Rita on the bus. I think it had something to do with the fact that, whenever some of the more frail and less mobile people were getting on or off the bus more slowly than Rita would have liked them to, she would scream at them and push them aside as she barged her way through. So it was not uncommon for our outings to begin and end with the bizarre ritual of everyone on the bus chanting, 'We hate you Rita! We hate you Rita! We hate you Rita!'

Now Evonne has always had a love for stray dogs, and indeed for underdogs of all kinds; and, because everyone we knew avoided Rita like the plague, Evonne went out of her way to get to know Rita. She began by dropping in to visit Rita at the hostel where she lived. And to begin with, Rita was not taken with Evonne. But Rita's eyes lit up when Evonne invited her out to the Café Babylon for coffee and cheesecake. Now Rita liked her biscuits; but she loved her cheesecake. And I think that it was by offering to treat her to cheesecake that Evonne won Rita's heart.

Each Tuesday morning, before going to art college, Evonne would drop into Rita's room at the hostel. Rita would be up, ready and waiting; dressed in her glad rags. When Evonne arrived they would help each other finish off the last touches of their make up; and, in spring, maybe even put a flower in their hair. Then they would be off. They made an odd couple: a happy twenty-year-old girl, with a bounce in her step, walking down the street with a crabby seventy-year-old woman shuffling along beside her, muttering every step of the way. But in time the locals got used to seeing this odd couple making their way to the café.

When they got to the Café Babylon the order would always be the same: coffee and cheesecake. To begin with Rita could barely contain her excitement about having a slice of cheesecake, and on occasions was known to jump the gun, and grab the slice of cheesecake sitting temptingly on a plate in front of another customer at a nearby table. Evonne would then have to restrain Rita while trying to calm an irate customer whose cheesecake had been eaten from under their eyes. However as time went by, Rita began to trust Evonne. If Evonne said Rita's cheesecake would come, it would come. She needn't snatch the first cheesecake she saw. Rita's cheesecake would come. Evonne would make sure of it. So Rita started to relax and learn to enjoy her coffee while waiting for her cheesecake.

Over coffee and cheesecake, bit by bit, Rita began to share her story with Evonne. When she was nineteen, Rita had been deemed a troublesome person, and sent to a local psychiatric hospital, where she had been confined for the next forty years. During that time she lost contact with all her family and her friends. She felt as if she actually had no family or friends; that the only one she could count on to look after her, was herself. So she learnt the skills she felt she needed to learn in order to survive in a cold, hard, clinical institution. She learnt to push. She learned to shove. She learned to fight. And she learned to grab as much as she could for herself, and shove it into her gob, before any one could come along and take it away from her. In the light of her story, suddenly it all made sense. Evonne understood Rita: understood her alienation, her anger, her strange, abnormal behaviour. And Rita knew Evonne understood.

Evonne and Rita became dear friends. When they talked, they laughed and cried. And after they laughed and cried, they danced. Not many people I know dance in coffee shops. In Brisbane, it's cool to dance in nightclubs, but it's not cool to dance in coffee shops. But after Evonne and Rita had bonded, Rita would often ask Evonne to dance with her round the tables and chairs of the Café Babylon. And though the customers found it rather strange, they didn't complain—as long as they got to eat their cheesecake in peace.

In the context of their friendship Rita began make some small but significant changes. The one I noticed was that she began to bum two cigarettes instead of one, off passers-by. When questioned as to why she wanted two cigarettes, Rita replied, 'I want one for me; and one for my friend, Evonne.' This was the first sign that I had ever seen of Rita showing any care for anyone else but herself, and it was a beautiful moment to behold.

Over the next few years Evonne and Rita spent a lot of time together. Not a little of it drinking coffee, eating cheesecake, and smoking the cigarettes they cadged. But their chats, though casual, were anything but idle. Through their conversations Rita reclaimed her soul. As their relationship bloomed, Rita seemed to blossom too. She remembered the songs of her youth; and she recovered her capacity to smile once again in her old age. She didn't do it often. She didn't want to overdo it. But when Rita did smile, it was as if Louis Armstrong had struck up the band, playing 'It's A Wonderful World', and all was well with the world at last.

One day, some time back, Rita had a stroke and was taken to hospital. Evonne was notified, and with Navi, she rushed to Rita's ward. When they arrived, Evonne and Navi were informed that the stroke had caused major damage, and that Rita was already brain-dead. The doctor told Evonne and Navi that they might as well go home, since there was nothing more they could do for Rita but turn off the life-support machine, and let her pass away. Evonne and Navi said they understood the situation, but they would not go home and leave Rita alone in hospital, as she had been before. They said Rita was their friend, and if she was going to die, they were going to make sure that she did not die alone. So Evonne stood on one side, and Navi stood on the other of the bed, and they held Rita's hands till she died.

A few months after the funeral, Evonne and I went for coffee and cheesecake at the Café Babylon for old times' sake. As we walked in, the waitress greeted Evonne like a long lost friend. Evonne introduced me to the waitress. Then the waitress said something I will never forget. She said, 'It's so nice to see Evonne again. We miss her so much. When she used to come here regularly, we loved it, because she used to bring her grandmother.' Evonne had related to Rita with such reverence that everyone in the café believed that Rita was actually a respected elderly member of our family. And so, I guess, she was.

Ideas for meditation, discussion, and action

Recall: When did we last feel compassion for someone?
Reflect: How—if at all—did we express our compassion?
Relate: What does the practice of true compassion mean to us?

5 Just Practice

Practising compassion, like Christ, involves practising principles that do justice to people. Principles are not a substitute for passions. Principles don't move us like passions do. But principles can guide our passions. Christ's principles can train us to develop our *passions* to be *com-passions*—feelings that take others' feelings into account. Christ's principles can teach us to be more truly and more thoroughly *com-passion-ate*—developing not only our capacity to feel other's feelings, but also our capacity to act with as much feeling for others' feelings as we do for our own.

Christ's principles give us a framework to help us think about what we feel about others. They help us test how we feel; help us check out our feelings; consider whether our feelings are real or not, and whether our feelings are relevant or not. Sometimes we feel as if we care for others, but our feelings are not real. They are fantasies, not realities. We are deluding ourselves. We all know it's a lot easier to pretend to care, than it is to care. Really caring hurts. Christ's principles give us a framework to test the reality of our compassion.

Sometimes we feel as if we care for others, and our feelings *are* real. They are realities, not fantasies. We are not deluding ourselves. We know how hard it is to care, and we do, we *really* do. It hurts. But really caring can do more harm than good, if it is not a *good* way of really caring. True care needs to be relevant as well as real. Christ's principles give us a framework to test the relevance, as well as the reality, of our compassion.

Christ shared his principles with his disciples through pithy sayings that were simple and practical: simple enough to

36

understand, and practical enough for anyone to be able to put them into practice.

> Don't make a show of your religion in order to attract attention to yourself. *Matthew 6:1*
>
> Whenever you do someone a favour, don't tell the world about it. *Matthew 6:2*
>
> Always treat other people as you would like them to treat you. *Matthew 7:12*
>
> Do not treat children with contempt. *Matthew 18:10*
>
> Treat older people with respect. *Luke 18:20*
>
> Just love your neighbour as yourself. *Luke 10:27*

Many of Christ's sayings reflect his concern that, in our love for others, we do justice to them—all of them; not just a favoured few, not a comfortable majority, but the whole community, including those that are usually most marginalised and disadvantaged.

> How sad it is for you who neglect to do justice. *Luke 11:42*
>
> What good will it do if you gain the whole world and lose your own soul? *Matthew 16:26*
>
> Unless your quest for justice gets beyond that of most of the religious people you know, you can't even begin to be involved in God's work in the world. *Matthew 5:20*
>
> Stop judging people by mere appearances. *John 7:24*
>
> Why don't you judge for yourself what is right? *Luke 12:57*
>
> Whoever wants to be a leader should be a servant of all. *Matthew 20:26*
>
> When someone invites you to a special function, do not take a place of honour. *Luke 14:8*

When you give a luncheon, do not invite your friends, or
relatives, or affluent neighbours. But when you give a banquet
invite the destitute, the disabled, the blind.   *Luke 14:12–13*

When Christ wanted to make sure his disciples remembered a
particularly important point he was trying to make, he would wrap
his pithy sayings in unforgettable punchy stories. One of the most
famous was a story he told to emphasise the importance of the
practice of justice in our ordinary everyday lives. We know this story
as the parable of the sheep and the goats.

> When the Human One comes, all the nations will be gathered
> before him, and he will separate the people one from another
> as a shepherd separates the sheep from the goats. He will
> put the sheep—who have done right—on his right, and the
> goats—who haven't—on his left. Then the True Leader will
> say to those on his right, 'Come, join the party. For I was
> hungry and you gave me a feed. I was thirsty and you gave
> me a drink. I had just arrived in town and you took me into
> your home. My clothes were in tatters and you gave me your
> own outfit. I was sick in bed and you came and spent time
> with me. I was stuck in prison and you were there for me
> and my family.' Stunned, the people on the right will say to
> him, 'When on earth did we see you hungry and give you a
> feed, or thirsty and give you a drink? When did we meet you
> after you had just arrived in town and give you a bed for the
> night? When were you sick in bed and we spent time with
> you? When were you stuck in prison and we were there for
> you and your family?' The True Leader will say, *'Whenever
> you did the right thing by those whom most consider least, you did the
> right thing by me!'* Then, turning to those on his left, the True

Leader will say, 'Get out. You can go to hell with everyone else who has made life hell for others. I was hungry and you never gave me a feed; thirsty and you never gave me a drink; lonely, without a friend, and you walked by; half-naked and you didn't give me any clothes; sick in bed, and stuck in jail, and you didn't even visit.' And those who are left will be bewildered, and say, 'When did we see you hungry or thirsty? When did we see you without a friend or without clothes? When did we see you sick in bed or stuck in prison?' And the True Leader will say to them, *'Whenever you did not do the right thing by those whom most consider least, you did not do the right thing by me!'*
  Matthew 25:31-46

The parable of the sheep and the goats is a classic Christ story. It lures an audience into listening to a harmless narrative, only to be led into a shocking encounter with a truth that is so frightening that they have been trying to avoid it all their lives. The shock in the story for the people in Christ's time, and for most Christians today, is that he insists that we will *not* be judged on the basis of whether we have subscribed to the right set of doctrines, or obeyed the right code of behaviour. *We will be judged solely on the basis of whether, or not, we have done the right thing by those whom most people consider least!*

Now some Christians argue that Christ *can't* be saying what he seems to be saying. He seems to be saying that we will be judged on the basis of the justice that we do, or do not do, to the disadvantaged. They say that 'we are saved by our relationship to Christ, not by our response to disadvantaged people'. But the whole point of the parable is that *the true nature of our relationship to Christ is demonstrated by our response to disadvantaged people*. We may claim to love Christ. Which is fine, fantastic. But in this parable, Christ says loud and clear that the only way that any of us can prove it is by our love for the poor!

There are some Christians who argue that this principle only applies to their treatment of their fellow-Christians. They say they will be judged on the basis of the way they treat poor Christians, but not on the basis of the way they treat poor non-Christians. But such an interpretation makes a complete mockery of this story. In the story, those whom we are expected to 'do the right thing by' are defined not in terms of their relationship to Christ, but in terms of their unmet needs. It is the hungry, the thirsty, the naked, the sick, and the imprisoned that Christ calls us to respond to, regardless of age, gender, colour, culture, or religion. The fact that Christ refers to those with unmet needs as his kin—and points out that he takes our treatment of these people very personally indeed—is only a further indication of just how strongly he feels about our doing justice to the disadvantaged.

We may say we have a passionate love for God and a compassionate love for our neighbours. We may mean what we say. But the principle Christ enunciated in the parable helps us understand exactly what a passionate love for God, and compassionate love for our neighbours, entails in our everyday lives. It means doing justice to all people, particularly those whom most consider least. To put this principle into practice we need to learn to relate to these people, whom most consider least; treat them as those whom we consider most; and help them meet their unmet needs.

This may seem very simple, but can be very difficult. Those whom most consider least are often very hard to find because, by their very definition, they are the people we usually ignore. Some we ignore, because we don't see them. Women battered secretly behind closed doors. Men sentenced to life behind prison or hospital walls. Seniors shut away in their own homes. People with disabilities, excluded from our workplaces, and our market places. Others we do see, but we ignore, because we don't see them as people 'like' us. We label them as old codgers, young punks, junkies, winos, bludgers, losers, fags, pimps, whores, crims, crazies, vegies, dagos, wogs, and boongs. And once we have labelled them as people 'unlike' us, we don't tend to relate to them as people 'like' us.

Then there are those we see as people like us, but because we see them as just the same as us, we ignore the differences. When we look at them we see ourselves, we do not see them as they really are. The neighbour we wave to every day, but whose anguish we know nothing about. The relative who cries in the privacy of their own room, over their continuing alienation from the family. The child we meet at the bus stop, who seems happy enough, but goes home to a living hell.

It is not easy to begin to relate to those in society whom most consider least, when we ourselves are to be numbered among the 'most' who 'consider them least'. We try to see them, but these people, and their pain, are hidden from our eyes by years of conditioning. I believe we can only begin to see those whom most— including ourselves—consider 'least', by looking for them through eyes of love.

I have a friend, Pippa, who lived in my neighbourhood for twenty years and swears she never saw an Aborigine. It's not that there weren't Aborigines around. In the middle of West End is Musgrave Park, which has served as a meeting place for Aborigines from southeast Queensland for hundreds, perhaps thousands, of years. And so around West End there are always mobs of *murris* (the word that local Aborigines use for their own people). But Pippa swears she never *saw* an Aborigine, till one day she was walking home from university, where for the first time in her life, she had attended a seminar run by an Aborigine whom she respected greatly. All of a sudden, her eyes were open, and she saw all these aborigines in the neighbourhood that she had never seen before. She only saw them by looking through eyes of love.

My wife Ange says it was pretty much the same for her as it was for Pippa. She grew up in West End, but never noticed disadvantaged people in our neighbourhood until she began looking round with eyes of love. Then she not only began to notice needy people on the streets; she also began to notice people with major unmet needs, on the edge of her own circle of acquaintances. As she began to relate to these people, Ange found her circle of concern continuing to expand—to include not only Aborigines, but also refugees; not only refugees, but asylum seekers; and not only asylum seekers, but also psychiatric survivors. Ange has found herself caught up in a centrifugal momentum of concern that has taken her further and further afield in wider and wider circles: to hospital and to prison, to nursing homes and to boarding houses, to rehabilitation centres and to sheltered workshops, to alleyways and to shooting galleries. And wherever she has gone, Ange has found herself face to face with people, and with their pain. Wherever the pain has been hidden, Ange has found that by developing relationships of trust, in which people feel safe enough to disclose their suffering, even strangers have been more than willing to share their struggle.

Once we have begun to develop face-to-face relationships with people whom most consider least, the question we are forced to ask ourselves is: are we going to engage with them in their struggle to survive, or not? If we want to live our lives like everyone else, then the chances are we simply won't have the time, or the energy, or the money, to invest in their struggle, even if we wanted to. The only way it is possible for us to have the time or the energy or the money to invest in their struggle is if we completely change the priorities that have hitherto governed our lives. And the only way we can do that, Christ says, is by literally putting the first last and the last first (Luke 13:30).

Normally we put *ourselves* first and *others* last. After all, that's conventional wisdom. Where we are concerned for others we usually put strong, intelligent, interesting, beautiful, rich, and famous people first, and weak, ignorant, boring, ugly, poor, and insignificant people last. After all, if we put ourselves out for others, we want to relate to those who will return our investment in them with dividends. And who better to return our investment in them, than strong, intelligent, interesting, beautiful, rich, and famous people? Where we are concerned for weak, ignorant, boring, ugly, poor, and insignificant people, we tend to put the ones that we feel hopeful about first, and the ones that we feel hopeless about last. After all, if we are going to go out of our way to help somebody, who wants to invest in someone who is not going to reward us with a sense of success? So we never get around to investing meaningfully in the lives of those whom most of us consider least. They are the last people we have in mind.

Christ says the only way we will ever have the time, and the energy, and the money, to invest meaningfully in the lives of those whom most, including ourselves, consider least, is by putting the first last and the last first. By taking the time we usually would invest in ourselves, and giving it to others. By taking the energy we would usually invest in the strong, intelligent, interesting, beautiful, rich, and famous, and giving it to the weak, ignorant, boring, ugly, poor, and insignificant. By taking the money we would usually invest in people that we feel hopeful about and giving it to people who we feel are hopeless!

Note, Christ is *not* saying, 'we should love others—not ourselves'. He is saying *'we should love others—as we love ourselves'*. We should recognise that few of us are actually as strong, or intelligent, or interesting, or beautiful, or rich, or famous as we would like to make out we are; most of us are actually more weak, and ignorant, and boring, and ugly, and poor, and insignificant than we would like to admit; so it is quite possible for those that are first, to love those that are last—*as we love ourselves*. But for those of us that are first, to do justice to those of us that are last, means for us to make a conscious decision to act contrary to the conventional wisdom of our society: by considering 'most', those whom most consider 'least'; by investing our time, our energy, and our money, in the lives of people whom we cannot expect to repay us, but who, unexpectedly, do—with interest; and by pouring ourselves into relationships that fail as often as they succeed, but never fail in helping us become the loving human beings we want to be.

When Ange and I got married, we decided that, as a couple, we would seek to put the first last and the last first. We weren't sure what that would mean for us at the time. It has meant different things for us at different times. At one stage it meant we felt we should sell everything we had—our house, our furniture, our car—and invest it in work with the poor in India. We felt we should work with people that no one would pay us to work for, and so we worked happily with disadvantaged people in India, as volunteers—supported only by the donations of family and friends—for twelve years.

Upon returning to Australia, we realised that we had to either rent a house, or buy one. Because we had already sold a house it seemed a contradiction for us to consider buying one. But the more we thought about it, the more we realised that, if we bought a house at the bottom end of the market, we would actually spend less money on accommodation than if we paid rent at market rates for the rest of our lives. So, while at an earlier stage we felt we should sell a house, at a later stage we felt we should buy one. By buying an old worker's cottage it meant we had to spend only a minimal amount of money on accommodation. That freed us to choose jobs that did not pay well, but provided an opportunity for us to work with the poor. It also freed us to choose part-time jobs, so that the rest of the time we could work without pay, for the poor who were not eligible for the services we could provide through our paid work. And when we eventually managed to buy a little old cottage, that the property agent said had 'a lot of potential', we made sure it was located in the West End area, so that we could be close to the disadvantaged people in the inner city with whom we feel called to share our lives.

In the story of the sheep and the goats, Jesus suggests that the way for us to do justice to the disadvantaged people that we share our lives with, is by making ourselves and our resources available to them, to help them meet their unmet needs. In the parable there is no suggestion of extraordinary people doing extraordinary things like healing the sick, or raising the dead, or single-handedly changing the course of human history. In the parable there is only the suggestion of ordinary people doing ordinary things for one another. Like giving someone a drink, or giving someone a feed, or spending time with someone sick in hospital or stuck in prison. For Jesus, doing justice is not about big people doing big things, but about little people doing little things to help one another. Doing justice is not about doing *great* things: it's about doing the *right* thing—simply helping one another.

Moving into West End has meant that Ange and I have been able to be involved more with disadvantaged people on a day-to-day basis. Some of the things that we do are quite complicated, but most of the things we do to help are simple things, that anyone could do. Ange often spends most of her day working with women at risk. I can recall a typical day some time back, when Ange was working for Salaam and ran into Leanne. Salaam is a refugee who was seeking asylum in Australia. She is from Eritrea, a small country on the Horn of Africa, which was at war with Ethiopia for more than twenty years, struggling for independence. Salaam's family was involved in the Eritrean Liberation Front, a political party that fought for independence, but is banned in Eritrea today. As a direct result of these political affiliations, Salaam's family have either fled into exile, or been killed. Salaam herself has been a refugee since she was ten years old. When she returned to Eritrea some years ago in search of members of her family who had disappeared, she was detained by the police. When they discovered her brother's affiliation with the Eritrean Liberation Front, they interrogated her for two days, during which time they raped her.

When Salaam was released, she fled to Saudi Arabia, where she got a job working with an Australian couple, with whom she later travelled to Australia. Upon her arrival she applied for a protection visa. But in spite of her vulnerability, the veracity of her story, and the fact there is no other country that she can go to, the Australian Government had refused Salaam the asylum she asked for on four occasions. So Ange, who is not a lawyer herself, spent much her day discussing the case with lawyers at the South Brisbane Immigration and Community Legal Service. Their advice to her was that, as all normal legal avenues of recourse were exhausted, Ange would need to appeal to the Minister of Immigration himself. With the help of Peter Noble, a lawyer friend in our community, who is committed to human rights, Ange set about writing a petition to the Minister, and organising a letter-writing campaign on Salaam's behalf.

While running round West End, organising the letter-writing campaign, Ange bumped into Leanne. Leanne is an Aboriginal woman who lives in West End. Leanne is pretty much apolitical. She isn't into campaigning. Not even for the rights of her own people. But Leanne wants *all* people—especially her own people—to be treated with respect. What Leanne wanted from Ange was just a few moments of her time: a smile, a chat, a cup of tea. And Ange, who loves Leanne, was more than happy to oblige. So in the middle of a frantic rush Ange was able to have a nice, quiet cup of tea with Leanne. Which, according to Ange, did her as much good as it did Leanne.

Jesus seems to suggest that we all have the capacity to meet the basic human needs of our neighbours. We can all give someone a cup of tea; we can all give someone a couple of sandwiches; we can all befriend someone who is lonely; and we can all take someone into our home, or help someone out who has hassles. The issue for Jesus, is not whether we *can* do justice to one another; but whether we *will,* or will not.

Ideas for meditation, discussion, and action

Recall: Who are the people in our community most consider least?

Reflect: How do we imagine Christ would want us to relate to these people?

Relate: What would it mean for us to make these people a priority in our lives?

6 Good Process

Practising compassion like Christ involves practising processes that are good for people: processes that people experience as good news, rather than bad news. We can all try to help people. But we need to recognise that not all attempts to help are helpful. In fact, some attempts to help can do more harm than good. Sometimes our attempts to help do not address the real need. We make assumptions about what is wrong. And we make assumptions about how to put it right. But we may miss the point completely. Just because we feel good about what we are doing doesn't necessarily mean we are doing anyone any good.

Even if we do address a real need, our manner may not be helpful. We may be patronising or condescending. So we may offer people some help, but our attitude may not be helpful. Even if our manner is helpful, our method may not be helpful. We may give advice when we should take action. So we give people a referral, but they can't follow up on it, because they need a lift, not just a referral. Our attempts to help people will only be helpful if they meet people's real needs, and do it in such a way as to build people up, and not put anyone down in the process. According to Christ, the very process we use should be 'good news to the poor'.

Christ advocated the utilisation of a range of processes that he considered were 'good news for the poor': relief, education, confrontation, development, and transformation.

- *Christ often took it upon himself to meet the needs of others*. He, and his disciples, actually gave regular gifts of money to people so their immediate needs could be met (John 12:4-6; 13:29). The process of emergency *relief* that Christ and his disciples practised was a simple transfer in cash or kind, with no strings attached, to anyone in need who asked for help. The best known case was when Christ was approached to provide food for a crowd of more than five thousand people who were desperately hungry because they had not eaten for three days. Though his disciples were daunted by the size of the request, Christ didn't hesitate. Refusing to send the crowd away hungry, Christ simply asked for donations of food, then began to distribute the bits of bread and pieces of fish that he was given, with a prayer on his lips that there would be enough to go round, and miraculously, so the story goes, there was more than enough for everyone! (Mark 6:37–44)

- *Christ also taught the community to meet their own needs.* The teaching of Christ, epitomised in the Sermon on the Mount, was a process of nonformal *education* that taught people that there would never be enough resources in the world to gratify anyone's greed, but there were more than enough resources in the world, if shared, to satisfy everyone's need. The classic example was Christ's encounter with Zacchaeus, the notorious tax collector. Over a meal together, Christ talked to Zacchaeus about the possibility of a community meeting its own needs, and the importance of people in the community like him playing their part in the process. As a result of his conversation with Christ, Zacchaeus was encouraged to renounce his greed, redistribute his riches to the poor so as to meet their needs, and make restitution to the community for the extortion he had committed (Luke 19:1-10).

- *Christ challenged all community groups to meet the needs in their communities, and confronted organisations that refused to play their part.* Christ turned the process of direct, public, nonviolent, political *confrontation* into an art form. The most famous of these confrontations was Christ's attack on the Temple in Jerusalem:

> One day, when Christ was in the Temple, he observed that the Court of the Gentiles was so crowded with Temple officials and their flunkies, that no Gentiles could get in. And what were these Temple officials and their flunkies doing? They were flogging off Temple sacrifices at vastly inflated, monopoly prices—exploiting the vulnerability of the worshippers who came from afar to offer their sacrifices of thanksgiving to God at the Great Temple in the Holy City.
>
> As he watched what was happening Christ became more and more angry. Here was exploitation of the worst kind—the religious authorities ripping off innocent believers in the name of God. So Christ overturned the tables of the merchants, and drove them out of the Temple with a rebuke ringing in their ears. 'This Temple was meant to be a place of prayer for people but you and your henchmen have turned it into the home cave of Ali Baba's forty thieves!'
>
> *Luke 19:45-46*

- *Christ developed an alternative model of community, in contrast to the dominant mode of operating in society that he denounced.* It was not good enough for him to criticise the injustice of the system; he felt he needed to demonstrate a process of community *development* that showed a way of structuring the political economy which did justice to the poor. The original model was the 'common purse'. Christ and his large band of at least seventy disciples shared a common purse. People contributed to the common fund as much as they could afford, and took from the common fund as much as they needed. After their expenses were paid for, the excess was shared with the poor. This was a revolutionary way of restructuring the political economy of a community which, if adopted by society, had the potential to meet the needs of everybody in the community, including people on the margins (John 12:4-6).

- *Christ encouraged a movement of people in society who would take the alternatives that he had developed with his disciples, and implement these principles, practices and processes in their lives individually and collectively without hesitation or reservation.* His prayer was for a process of total *transformation* of society. He not only prayed for this himself; he taught his disciples to pray earnestly for the day when God's would be 'done, on earth, as it is in heaven'. The day when all debts would be cancelled, all wage slaves would be set free, and all men and all women would be able to meet all the basic human needs of their families.

In those early years the church was a movement of people who took the alternatives that Christ had developed with his disciples, and began to implement these principles, practices and processes in their community. Not without hesitation or reservation, but haltingly, and falteringly, these people opened themselves to the Spirit of Christ, and to the incredible possibility Christ espoused, that they as ordinary people could actually transform society. They took the co-operative approach of the common purse and applied it to a whole range of personal, social, and economic issues in their communities. They devoted themselves to relationships, to sharing meals with each other, and to praying for one another. They were all together with sincere hearts. They had everything in common. Even their possessions were held in trust for one another. Whenever it was necessary, people would sell their possessions, and give to anyone as they had need, so *there wasn't anyone with an unmet need!* (Acts 2:43-45; 4:32-34)

These days, certain groups of people seem to favour one kind of process over another, regardless of the issue they are addressing. Charitable groups usually opt for relief; religious groups usually opt for education; and radical groups usually opt for confrontation. Rarely do these groups consider the other options available. All the types of processes have their time and place. So whenever we are confronted with a issue we must carefully choose which of the processes is most appropriate for resolving a particular problem. Relief may be helpful in a crisis, but actually may be counterproductive in normal circumstances. Education may not be helpful in a crisis, but may be much more helpful in normal circumstances, unless the issue is injustice, rather than ignorance, in which case confrontation may be more appropriate. It may be that a number of options—indeed a combination of options—need to be adopted in order to address the issues we are confronted with in the community.

But I've noticed there is a tendency for different people to avoid different processes. All of us, it would seem, are predisposed towards certain types of processes, and against other types of processes, because of our personalities. Yet I suspect there are often deeper reasons we avoid certain types of processes. Some of us avoid relief because we do not really want to share our own hard-earned resources to meet other people's needs. We will only be free to opt for emergency relief if we recognise that other people have as much right to our hard-earned cash as we have. A few of us avoid education because training others to meet their own needs usually involves a long-term, rather than a short-term commitment. We will only be free to opt for education if we are prepared to invest the same time training people in life skills that others have invested in us.

Many of us avoid confrontation because we are afraid of conflict, preferring the support of the power-brokers for our charitable work rather than risking their opposition by exposing their manipulation of the people we are working with. We will only be free to opt for confrontation if we join the ranks of those who are willing to suffer at the hands of the power-brokers for their stand against institutionalised injustice. Many of us may avoid development because we would prefer to put the onus for change onto others rather than ourselves. It always has been and always will be easier to criticise others than it is to change ourselves. We will only be free to opt for development if we realise that the only way we can change the world is to change our own way of life. Most of us avoid transformation because we want to give people a hand but we are wary about letting things 'get out of hand', at least out of our hands, and the work of regeneration will always be out of our hands. We will only be free to opt for transformation if we are willing to work hand in hand with others, allowing them to set the agenda for our involvement.

I constantly struggle to respond to the issues in my community with due process. Take an issue like accommodation. It's a major problem in our neighbourhood. There are always people in our area looking for places to stay, and there never seem to be enough suitable places available at affordable prices. Each person who phones me up asking for a place to stay represents a terrible dilemma for me. Sometimes I feel I just can't cope, and I say I can't help. Sometimes I want to help, but I'm not sure what to do. Should I offer them emergency accommodation, or not? If they need just a few days we can often accommodate people. But do they really need accommodation, or do they need some education about how they can manage their budget better, so they can pay their rent on time next time and not get evicted? Then again, maybe they don't need any education at all. Maybe they are good tenants. Maybe their landlord is a bad landlord. Maybe he has evicted them for no good reason. Maybe it's the landlord that needs to be taught a lesson, not the tenant. Maybe it's time for action. However, quite frankly, I am tired of confrontation. So many fights over so many years, and so little to show for the scars. Maybe we need to put less time into disputes over insecure accommodation and more time into developing secure accommodation through public housing, co-housing, and housing co-operatives. But I know I'm living in fantasyland if I think working with co-operatives is going to mean less fighting. It may mean less fighting with our enemies, but it will mean *more* fighting with our friends. Our only long-term hope is transformation. So how do I do justice to the person asking for a place to stay, waiting for a reply on the other end of the phone?

I believe that it is only as I am truly free in my spirit, like Christ, that I can be flexible enough to embrace the most appropriate process—or the most appropriate combination of processes—to address the issues raised in any given situation. And as there is no good process without due process, I faithfully seek to practise due process, in spite of my fears.

The phone rings and John says he is coming to town, needs a bed for a couple of nights, but has no money to pay for a place. Can he stay for the weekend? *Sure.* We have a spare bed for a couple of nights, he can stay for the weekend .The phone rings again and Janice says her husband is on the booze again, and has beaten her up again. Can she come and stay with us for a while? *Probably.* But we should have a talk to her about the need for her to stand up for herself, and finally give that brute of a husband of hers the flick, once and for all. Janice needs to think about getting some permanent accommodation of her own, not taking some temporary accommodation like John. The phone rings once again and Jameel says that he has been to every real estate agent in town and can't get a house to rent, and he's starting to get the idea that there's plenty of apartments for whites, but there's no room for blacks. Can we do a round of the real estate agents with him and advocate on his behalf? *You bet*. Most of the real estate agents in our part of town are Greek. So most of them are Orthodox. Jameel is not Greek. But he is Orthodox. There are going to be plenty of discussions about the relationship between Orthodoxy and humanity—and racist attitudes in real estate—before the day is over and we say *adios*.

The phone rings yet again and Jamie says they are having another fight in the housing co-op. Can I come over to his place to talk about it? Sort out some kind of strategy together so he can do something about it? Silence. A couple of big, deep breaths as I psych myself up to face another round of conflict. *Let's do it*. After all the co-op are a great crew, providing good quality long-term accommodation to heaps of vulnerable people in the neighbourhood—black and white alike—according to priority of need. It's a tough and thankless job. And they often get taken for granted. Hence the conflict over a member who believes that the co-op exists purely to meet his personal needs. It is time for everybody in the co-op to get together and call the careless member to account. The phone rings one more time. I pick it up. It's Jason. He sounds like Jesus. I don't know why, but he always sounds like Jesus. Jason-Jesus simply says: *Hang in there buddy!*

What reason have I got to hang in there? Well, come to think of it, I guess I have a few. There's Neil and Penny, round the corner, who have provided a home for two young boys whom they have adopted, and at the same time have cared for their mother, who has been suffering with chronic dementia, at home, for the last five years. Then there's Rono and Collette, down the road, who with a dedicated circle of friends, have provided a secure home environment, with a carefully constructed network of special support, for their son Liam who has struggled with cerebral palsy for the last twenty years. And then there's Kimberly who lived in institutions most of her early life, got out in order to get a place of her own in the community, only to be kicked from pillar to post as a tenant, till she managed to get the independent unit of her dreams, provided by a progressive government housing project, and is now living more or less happily ever after. To me, these people are signs of hope that the transformation of the community that we all pray for is not a complete impossibility after all.

Ideas for meditation, discussion, and action

Recall: What is the most crucial issue our community needs to deal with?

Reflect: Which process might be the most appropriate to deal with this issue?

Relate: How do we imagine things might change if we acted on this issue?

7 Strong but Gentle Power

Practising compassion, like Christ, involves developing power that is strong but gentle with people. Power that is strong but gentle *with* people is not power that is exercised *over* people, but power that people exercise over themselves. The power that is strong but gentle with people is power that essentially comes from *within* a person or a group of persons.

Yet nearly every time I talk with people about developing a project in their community, the conversation quickly turns from talk about *internal* sources to *external* sources of power. If they want to organise a welfare programme, they want to talk about funds. 'Where can we get the funds we need to run the programme?' they inquire. If they want to organise a protest movement, they want to talk numbers. 'How can we get the numbers we need to get a major social movement on a roll?' they ask. These reactions reveal that people, both on the right and on the left of the political spectrum, believe that external resources matter more than internal sources of power. They believe that we can only do significant work in our community if we have access to either lots of cash, or large crowds, or both. It becomes all about fund-raising and number-crunching.

So many communities disempower themselves because they frame their problems, and the solutions to their problems, in terms of access to resources, which by definition are beyond their control. If they can't get access to the resources they require in order to act, they simply do not act. If they do get the resources they require, they may act, but only according to the terms and conditions that have been set for the support they receive. Either way, they abrogate their power to solve their own problems; they project the power to solve their problems onto others; and in so doing, they render themselves powerless.

Christ challenged people's dependence on external resources for community work. On two occasions he sent his disciples out into various villages to do community work. On the first occasion, he forbade them to take any money at all. According to Christ, money was not essential for community work: it was a merely a note promising to share a certain amount of commodities or services. What mattered to Christ, was not that his disciples carried a note that held the promise of help, but that his disciples actually helped the people they met, out of the people's own internal resources. On the second occasion he allowed them to take a little money, but not much. According to Christ, money was never to be considered a *primary source*, but only a *secondary resource*. External resources like money could be helpful as a secondary resource for community work. But if external resources ever became a substitute for internal sources, and money became a primary rather than secondary consideration, then Christ warned us that money would not only destroy our work, but also our community. After all, 'the love of money is the source of evil' (1 Timothy 6:10).

On both the occasions Christ sent his disciples out to do community work, he didn't send them out in big numbers, and he didn't expect them to get big numbers involved. It was less a mass movement, more a micro movement. He didn't send his disciples out in their hundreds, or thousands, but in twos. And he didn't expect them to get hundreds or thousands involved, but one here, and one there. As far as Christ was concerned, two meeting one and forming a group of three was a big enough crowd to begin to overthrow the order of the day. For Christ a trinity was not so much a theological abstraction as it was a strategy for developing true community in society. A group of three could create *within* themselves the stability and security necessary for any development. 'A cord of three strands is not easily broken' (Ecclesiastes 4:12). A group of three could create within themselves the subjectivity and objectivity necessary for community development. 'Let every matter be decided on the basis of two or three witnesses' (Matthew 18:16). And a group of three could create within themselves the time and space necessary for Christ-like community development. 'Wherever two or three of you gather in my name', Christ said, 'there am I in the midst of you' (Matthew 18:20). According to Christ, a small, apparently insignificant group of just three people can have all the internal resources they need to create a significant movement in society towards community.

Most attempts to bring about change in society haven't come unstuck because the groups involved lacked the funds or the numbers. Most came unstuck because of power struggles that caused the groups to self-destruct. The people in the group lacked the power to change themselves, let alone their society. Christ taught that the most important single issue in bringing about change, was for groups to discover the power to manage their affairs in a way that gave everyone a fair go—power that enabled them to transcend their selfishness, resolve their conflicts, and deal with their issues in a way that did justice to everybody involved. Without that strong but gentle power, Christ said, we should not even try to start working for change, lest we end up destroying the world that we are trying to create (Luke 24:49). However, with that strong but gentle power, Christ said, nothing on earth can stop us from building a better world—neither lack of funds, nor lack of numbers; nothing (Matthew 17:20). So when Christ sent his disciples out to build a better world, he imparted to them what he called 'the power of the Spirit' (John 20:21–22). This Spirit was 'not a spirit of timidity, but of power, characterised by discipline of self, and compassion for others' (2 Timothy 1:7). So as they opened themselves to this Spirit, it produced in them the strong but gentle power to control themselves, and to love others as they loved themselves.

Now most people who have been involved in trying to bring about change in the world, would find it easy to accept Christ's idea that power was the most important single issue in the process. But many would find it more difficult to accept the kind of power, the power of the Spirit, that Christ advocated. Not merely because of the spiritual language Christ used to describe his idea of power, but because of the substantial difference between the dominant notion of power, to which many of us subscribe, and his alternative notion.

There are two ways of understanding power. Our traditional understanding of power has been defined as the ability to control other people. It emphasises the possibility of bringing about *change through coercion*—an approach that tries to make others change according to our agendas. While this traditional, dominant notion of power involves taking control of our lives by taking control of others, Jesus advocated a radical alternative: taking control of our lives, not by taking control of others, but by taking control of ourselves. This alternative emphasises bringing *change by conversion*— an approach that does not try to make others change, but tries to change ourselves, individually and collectively, in the light of a glorious agenda for justice. It breaks the control that others have over us, and liberates us from our desire to control others.

The dominant notion of power is popular because it often brings quick, dramatic results. But it is characterised by short-term gains for some, and long-term losses for everyone else. Every violent revolution in history, has sooner or later betrayed the people in whose name it fought its bloody war of liberation. The alternative notion of power is unpopular because it is usually a slow, unspectacular process. But it is the only way for groups to transcend their selfishness, resolve their conflicts, and manage their affairs in a way that does justice to everyone.

The essential problem in any situation of injustice is that one human being is exercising control over another and exploiting the relationship of dominance. The solution to the problem is not simply to reverse roles, in the hope that once the roles have been reversed, the manipulation will cease. The solution is for people to stop trying to control each other. All of us, to one degree or another, exploit the opportunity if we have control over another person's life. Common sense therefore dictates that the solution to the problem of exploitation cannot be through the dominant approach to power, with its emphasis on controlling others. The solution is in the alternative, the strong but gentle approach, which emphasises controlling ourselves, individually and collectively, through self-managed processes and structures.

Some of us sincerely believe that if we are to help people, particularly the oppressed, we need to manage their affairs for them. But no matter how we try to rationalise it, controlling others always empowers us and disempowers those we seek to help. The only way people can be helped, particularly the oppressed, is for them to be empowered to take control over their own lives. This is why Christ explicitly forbade his followers taking control over others, no matter how dire the circumstances. Their job was not to seek control, but to enable others to take control over their own lives (Matthew 20:25–28). It is a pity that many of us who claim to follow Christ have not followed his advice. We could have been saved the crusades and the inquisition. It is a great irony to me that the greatest example we have in modern times of someone who did act on Christ's advice, did not claim to be a Christian. We need a lot more people like Gandhi who will experiment with the nonviolent revolution of *swaraj* or self-rule.

It's interesting to note that Christ and his disciples used organic images to describe how the power of the Spirit, the secret of *swaraj*, actually operates in our lives. Self-management is described as the 'fruit of the Spirit' (Galatians 5:22). The capacity to manage ourselves develops quite unobtrusively—indeed, as quietly as fruit growing on a tree. But though it may develop unobtrusively, it is far more significant than we might ordinarily imagine. Like a minute seed, so small we can scarcely see it, that seems like it could never amount to anything great, the power of the Spirit seems embarrassingly insignificant to begin with, yet grows into a capacity that is of tremendous significance in the end (Matthew 13:31–32). The capacity to control our own lives does not develop without opposition, but like a plant growing in the midst of weeds, the power of the Spirit grows strong in an environment that could easily destroy it (Matthew 13:24–30). How these seeds of transformation grow in a community, always was and always will be a mystery (Mark 4:26–29). However, it is no secret that the seeds of transformation that bear the fruit of the Spirit will not grow in a community, if those of us whose lives constitute those seeds do not bury ourselves in the life of our community. 'Unless a seed falls into the ground and dies it produces nothing, but if it dies it will produce much fruit, that brings much life to others' (John 12:24).

I must admit that to the uninitiated this does sound a bit like mystical nonsense. It is mystical, that's for sure. But it's not nonsense. It actually works in the nitty-gritty of real life. When Ange and I started to get involved in West End, we began as a couple by trying to find at least one other person whom we could link up with, so the three of us as a group could have within ourselves, the personal and relational resources that we needed in order to work towards developing community in our locality. As it turned out we found not one person but two, a couple by the name of Chris and Ruth Todd, who had moved into the area with the intention of getting involved in developing community in the locality themselves. We had no external resources at all, only our internal resources: our time, our energy, our knowledge, our skills, and our love. We had no plans, no projects, no programmes. Just the hope that, together, we might be able to find a way of developing a Christ-like life in the community; a lifestyle characterised by the radical, nonviolent, sacrificial compassion of Christ; distinguished by commitment to love and to justice; working from the bottom up to empower people, particularly the marginalised and disadvantaged; so as to enable them to realise their potential, as men and women, made in the image of God; through self-directed, other-orientated intentional community processes and structures. It sounds like a pretty grand vision. But it was more a passion than a vision. Because we didn't have a clue what to do, or how to do it.

So Chris, Ruth, Ange, and I began to meet regularly for prayer: praying that God would fill us with the strong but gentle power of the Spirit, so we could respond to the plight of the people around us appropriately. Slowly but surely, the dream of the West End Waiters' Union began to emerge, and as we discussed it with others, a few friends gathered round in the hope that perhaps together we could make this dream come true. We decided to call ourselves the West End Waiters' Union because we wanted to be 'waiters' in West End. We didn't want to set agendas for people. We just wanted to be available, like waiters, to take people's orders, and to do what we could do to help them. We particularly wanted to help to develop a sense of hospitality in the locality, so that all people, especially people who are usually displaced in areas like ours, could really begin to feel at home in the community.

There have never been many people in the Waiters' Union. We started with two households fifteen years ago; there aren't more than twenty households associated with us now. The Waiters' Union is not a high-profile group. As waiters, we try to keep a low profile in the area. None of the activities that we are involved in carry our name. They all carry the names of the groups that organise those activities, which we contribute to but do not control.

As a result, many people in our area may know us well as people, but may not even know that the group we are part of exists. Which is fine, because the group exists to promote the community, not the group; and the group can function more effectively as a catalyst in the community if it is prepared to be more or less invisible, rather than attract attention to itself at the expense of other groups. However, we are not secretive. We welcome enquiries and answer questions as freely and as fully as we can. And we are inclusive. We invite anyone who is interested in our work to work with us, alongside of us, as partners in the work together.

All the work we do is *self-directed* and *other-orientated*. Each person has the right to shape every group that they are a part of. Being part of a group depends on participation. A person becomes a part of a group, not by jumping through any hoops, but simply by participating in the group. Once a person is a part of the group, they have the right to manage that group. We believe people have the right to shape all the decisions that impact on their lives. And we believe the best way for us to shape these decisions, individually and collectively, is through the process of consensus. So all the groups nominate rotating facilitators for their meetings so as to be careful to do what, as the good book says, 'is right in the eyes of everybody' (Romans 12:17). As the groups work from the bottom up, to empower people, particularly people who are marginalised and disadvantaged, we particularly include people who are usually marginalised and disadvantaged in the decision-making process of the groups. So all the groups actually work *with* the people that they work *for*, and, in so doing, seek to enable the people they work with, as partners, to realise their enormous potential as men and women made in the image of God.

Through one group, we seek to promote the aspirations of the original inhabitants of our neighbourhood, for whom Musgrave Park, in the middle of the neighbourhood, is still sacred ground. Through another group, we seek to support refugees by sponsoring their settlement and the settlement of their families, working through the anguish they go through as strangers in a strange land. Last, but not least—though they are often considered last, and treated as least by the powers that be—through a whole range of groups, we seek to relate to the physically, intellectually, and emotionally disabled people in our community: not as 'clients', nor as 'consumers', still less as 'users', but as our friends! None of these things seem that great. However, we constantly encourage one another to remember that true greatness is not in doing big things, but in doing little things with a lot of love over the long haul. And that is exactly what we are trying to do.

The Waiters' Union has always been a nonformal community network. But over time we have come to recognise the need for a formal community organisation as an auspice for some of our community activities. Usually groups solve this problem by turning their nonformal community network into a formal community organisation. But, in the move towards institutionalisation, they lose the very charisma of community. The free and flexible, strong but gentle spirit of the community that they started out with, ends up being bound hand and foot by rules and regulations and becoming a slave to the system that it sought to overthrow.

So we decided that we would not institutionalise our community under any circumstances, but set up a formal organisation as a parallel structure alongside the nonformal network, so that if anyone in the community needed an officially-recognised, legally-registered auspice for certain activities, they could use the 'Community Initiatives Resource Association'. To make sure the Resource Association only serves as an auspice for the Waiters' Union, and does not have the power to co-opt the Waiters' Union, it has been designed as a minimalist organisation, with minimal power apart from its capacity to function as an official, legal auspice for the community.

Since its inception the Resource Association has provided an auspice for managing community property, providing compulsory public liability insurance, and supplying volunteers with the status required by the state. But by far the association's greatest role has been to help establish community programmes which needed legal backing for funding, with maximum accountability but minimal control. The Resource Association has helped establish everything from the Creative Stress Solutions Project, to the Inner City Citizens' Advocacy Group, through to the Praxis Community Co-operative.

In June 2000 a bunch of us were asked to help out in one of the outlying caravan parks. In spite of romantic associations with the name, few of the caravan parks ringing the city of Brisbane serve as happy way stations for passing gypsies. The residents we met called them 'dumps', referring to themselves as 'trailer trash.' Sunnybank Family Support, who had contact with the people in the Sunnybank Caravan Park, were concerned for the welfare of the residents and asked Jim, Pete and me if there was anything we could do to help them develop a positive sense of community in the park. We thought we could, so said we'd give it a go.

Jim negotiated entry with the management and started to visit the park in July, wandering round the sites and getting into conversations with the residents. To begin with most of the residents were pretty suspicious, but as the month went by and Jim came by regularly two or three times a week, they began to trust him. By August Jim was able to organise a meeting with the residents to talk about the kind of things they would like to do to improve their life in the park. They dreamt up heaps of good ideas, but didn't feel they were up to making them a reality. So they asked Jim if he could arrange some training to give them some basic skills.

From September through to November Pete and I ran a course with Jim called 'Building A Better Community' in the annex of one of the caravans in the park. We met once a week over lunch for three hours, discussing our hopes for the community and ways of overcoming barriers that had blocked progress in the past, how to run groups, how to manage conflict, and how to solve problems. In December the residents took their first tentative steps towards starting a small savings and loan co-op in order to deal with their ongoing financial difficulties. Jim linked them up with a resource person, from a local agency that worked in micro-finance, who provided the expert advice they needed to get established.

In the last week of January the residents opened a joint co-op bank account. In the meantime, with the support of the staff from Sunnybank Family Support, they had also set up a craft group, a food bank, several car pools, special men's and women's groups, and published a park resource directory!

In February Jim finished his work at Sunnybank Caravan Park. But in March he was invited by the residents to go to the National Caravan Park Workers Seminar where they were asked as a group, to tell the story of the work they had done. Jim said that he sat there in sheer amazement as he heard the residents talk with enthusiasm about their experience. About how they had been able to rediscover their confidence, 'come together' and 'work together', and 'really change things'.

So the strong but gentle revolution rolls on.

Ideas for meditation, discussion, and action

Recall: Where have we seen strong but gentle power at work?

Reflect: What difference does the 'power of the Spirit' make?

Relate: How can we develop power with people in our community?

A Heart for Breaking Barriers

May your strength increase.
    May courage never cease.
May your confidence never ever falter.

May your vision be true.
    May your wisdom always do.
May your knowledge always take you further.

May your love for God be sure.
    May your love for forgotten people always endure.
May the wonder come.
    May heaven's work on earth be done.
Through you and your family—forever.

'Forever' from the album Wonder Come *by Dave Andrews*

8 Breaking Barriers of Futility

At the heart of humanity lies hope: a hope that is as necessary for our survival as earth, air and water. At the heart of hope is a dream: a dream that something, somewhere, some time will change.

We dream of a world in which all the resources of the earth will be shared equally between all the people of the earth so that even the most disadvantaged among us will be able to meet their basic needs with dignity and joy. We dream of a great society of small communities interdependently cooperating to practise individual, socio-economic, and political righteousness and peace. We dream of networks of neighbourhoods where people can really relate to one another as neighbours. We dream of circles of friends where the pain people carry deep down can surface, and be shared openly in an atmosphere of acceptance and respect. We dream of community groups and organisations where people can begin to explore the difficulties they have in common, discern the problems, discover the solutions, and work together in a spirit of compassion for personal and social change that reflects the revolutionary agenda of Jesus Christ. And those of us who are Christians dream of every church, in every locality, acting as a catalyst to make this dream a reality.

But if we have ever tried to break a habit ourselves, tried to help a friend break an addiction, or tried to break through the walls of vested interest that stand in the way of social justice, then we will have discovered that at the heart of the battle there is always the fight with an overwhelming sense of futility. Established patterns of personal and social behaviour are extremely difficult to change, and are even more excruciatingly difficult to continue to keep changing in a way that reflects a genuine ongoing struggle for justice. So people who struggle for change constantly find themselves face to face with impregnable, intransigent, cultural fortresses, built firmly on the foundation of misplaced traditions of obedience, desires for approval, fears of punishment, hopes of reward, and bouts of laziness, that are almost impossible to change.

Others have tried to break through these barriers before us. We have tried to break through these barriers ourselves, only to end up disconsolately sitting on the floor, surrounded by wish lists, tied up in red tape, suffering from a terrible headache as a result of trying to bash our heads against one brick wall after another.

I telephoned the pastor of a local church when we were trying to get involved in the local community, and I asked him about the possibility of maybe getting his congregation involved with us in some community work in our neighbourhood. I'd barely got the question out, when he answered, 'Not a chance!' He went on to explain, 'Most of the people in the church don't live in this area, and would not be interested in being involved in the area. Those who might be interested are so busy with church activities they wouldn't have time anyway. They won't even open the door of their house to me, their pastor, let alone a stranger!'

In so saying, the pastor expressed a sense of futility that we all feel, from time to time, when we attempt to persuade the people in the cultural fortresses around us to open their lives to one another, and they show no interest at all. At that moment, I felt the pastor's sense of futility myself. It's pretty discouraging when you knock on the door of a castle to say 'G'day' to your neighbours, only to have the hired help pull up the drawbridge, and drop the portcullis in your face.

Christ faced this same sense of futility. On one occasion, a rich young man came to Christ asking what he could do to help his cause. 'Sell all you have and give the money to the poor,' was Christ's response. The rich young man just turned on his heels and walked away. Christ looked at his quizzical disciples, and told them that they should never ever think that it would be easy to get rich people involved with the poor. He quipped, 'It is easier to squeeze a camel through the eye of a needle, than it is for the rich to get involved in God's movement that seeks to do justice to the poor!' Christ knew full well the futility of trying to convince the rich to share their wealth with the poor. But he still did it. The futility didn't make him flinch. It seemed like an impossible dream. But Christ simply refused to accept it as impossible. 'What we usually consider *impossible*,' he said to his disbelieving disciples, ' believe it or not, is *possible* with God' (Luke 18:27).

As far as Christ was concerned, the impossible was really possible after all. It was possible for the impossible dream of the rich sharing their wealth with the poor to come true. But as far as the disciples were concerned this was just a completely utopian dream. And while they believed it was an impractical, unrealistic, idealistic dream, it remained one. It was only when the disciples began to act on the possibility that the impossible was possible, that the completely utopian dream became an eminently, and immanently, practical reality. As the Spirit came upon the dispirited disciples, it actually began to happen, the rich began sharing their wealth with the poor— voluntarily! In the church community in Jerusalem, the rich even sold their possessions and shared the proceeds with the poor. Luke, in his record of those days, says, 'No one claimed that any of their possessions was their own, but they shared everything they had' to such an extent that 'there wasn't a needy person left among them' (Acts 2:43–47, 4:32–37).

While it is true that dreams can be transformed into reality, we must beware of naïveté—of belief without doubt, which ignores the facts, and lives in a world of foolish optimism. I can remember the time I believed I could change the world, all by myself. I was optimistic. But my optimism blinded me to the essence of the struggle for change. We must grow beyond such naïve optimism. At the same time we must beware of cynicism—of doubt without belief, which rejects faith altogether, and lives in a world of futile pessimism. I can remember the times I doubted the world could ever be changed. I couldn't even change myself, let alone the world! My pessimism debilitated me, sapping the strength I needed for the struggle for change. We must not only grow past naïve optimism. We must also grow past cynical pessimism if we want to change the world.

One of the things that disturbs me most is that many of us have our naïve optimism knocked out of us very quickly. Our naïve optimism is replaced by a cynical pessimism, and every knock we take from then on reinforces an increasing sense of scepticism. Some of us never get out of it; we are left paralysed by an overwhelming sense of pointlessness. We need to learn to grow into a new level of maturity: a maturity which neither rejects faith in the possibility of change, nor ignores the facts that say change is impossible; which acknowledges the difference between dreams and realities, yet recognises the difference God can make in turning utopian dreams of true community into practical reality. We must learn to live as if the impossible is possible. Though there are no guarantees that everything will change if we do, it is absolutely certain that nothing will change if we don't.

Some cynics may tell me that I am naïve in believing that the impossible is possible. But I don't think I am naïve. Because there are many times I have doubted we could change our world. But in spite of these doubts, I have continued to believe that we could live our lives in such a way as to bring about change. And the impossible has actually happened. Over and over again, my wife and I and our friends have done things that have brought about real change in our world. My wife says we have changed: maybe not a lot, but at least a little. And my friends say the changes that we have made in our family have helped us change our community: maybe only partially, and temporarily, but significantly nonetheless. The cynics would no doubt say that for me to believe this proves I am naïve! Maybe I am. If so, so be it. I would prefer to be a naïve fool who at least tries to do something that ought to be done, than to be a cynical sage who does nothing but criticise those who try.

In spite of the pastor telling me about the impossibility of getting people from the church involved in the community in our area, I persisted. I knew that it would be hard to get comfortable people involved in the uncomfortable process of community development. But I didn't give up; I kept on going. Sure, doors were shut in my face. But I was determined to 'keep on knocking'. For Christ says, 'if you keep on knocking, sooner or later, the doors will open' (Matthew 7:7). Whenever there was half an opening, I talked to people about the prospect of being involved in our community. Many rolled their eyes at me dismissively. But I was determined to 'keep on asking.' For Christ says, 'if you keep on asking, eventually someone will give you the very thing you were asking for all along' (Matthew 7:7). And eventually people did respond, a person here, a couple there.

Don and Fay Lovett were a relatively wealthy middle-class couple whom we talked to about getting involved with the poor in our community. But they remained more or less preoccupied with their own private world, until one day, Don found himself in a hospital bed with a potentially life-threatening brain tumour. As he lay there, Don recalled the conversations that he'd had with Ange and me, about getting involved in the community. And he realised that, after all he'd said he would do, he had never got around to doing anything, and now it was probably too late to do anything. Don talked it over with Fay, and they decided, that if he survived, he would not go back to full-time work, but work part-time, dedicating the rest of his time to befriending lonely people in our locality. As it happened, to Fay's great delight, Don did survive. They felt like they had been given another chance. And they were determined to use the extra time they had been given as well as they could. So Don and Fay Lovett spent the rest of their life together as a couple unpretentiously serving destitute people in our neighbourhood. Doing the very thing that the pastor had told me it was impossible for me to expect them to do.

Ideas for meditation, discussion, and action

Reflect: What do we imagine is God's dream for our community?

Relate: How could we possibly make a dream like that come true?

Respond: What actions are we willing take to make that dream a reality?

9 Breaking Barriers of Selfishness

Our culture celebrates selfishness. 'You've got to look after self', we say. 'If you don't look after yourself no one else will!' Our philosophy can be summed up best in the popular slogans that are doing the rounds of the cocktail-party circuit. 'Greed is good!' 'If you want it, get it!' 'Buy now, pay later!' Our political economy is a capitalist economy,.based on capital as the means of production and consumption of goods and services. Money is the currency required to purchase these goods and services. And the market is the mechanism for distributing the goods and services that are purchased. Those with a lot of money get lots of goods and services. Those with a little money get little goods and services. And those with no money get nothing. We say we believe in charity. But we believe that 'charity begins at home'. And that being so, charity seldom extends much further than our own families.

Christians profess to be different, but often display the same self-centredness. Some time back I was talking to a young lady from a trendy, suburban church. She was extraordinarily animated. What amazed me, was that she oozed with enthusiasm for life. But what worried me, was that her enthusiasm was focused entirely on her *own* life. She was completely preoccupied with herself—her business and her success in her business. Unfortunately, this young woman typifies the self-involved spirituality that is rampant in far too many trendy, suburban churches: a spirituality that prays for a parking space, but drives past poor people stranded in the rain. I tried to talk to this young woman about her self-involved spirituality. But she got mad at me, stormed out of the room, and sped off in her brand new BMW.

Christ said that if we want to be committed to living a life that is dedicated to people, apart from ourselves, we need to make some serious decisions about our lifestyle. Christ insists we need to reject our role as passive consumers in a passive consumer society. He says 'do not keep worrying about what you are going to eat or what you are going to drink' (Matthew 6:25). That's not the issue. The issue is that we all need to stop eating and drinking to excess, and to start hungering and thirsting for justice (Matthew 5:6). Justice will never be done in our communities by eating Big Macs and drinking cans of Coke, sitting in front of the television watching a documentary on street kids. Justice will only ever be done by turning off the television, getting off our butts, meeting the kids on the street, and inviting them home for a family meal. Not as fellow consumers; but as brothers and sisters.

Our selfishness cannot be dealt with by engaging in analysis of self. The irony is that any effort to deal with selfishness by introspection only makes us more selfish. We become preoccupied with our own improvement as a person and that is essentially a selfish process. Selfishness can only be dealt with by giving up our preoccupation with ourselves and giving ourselves, wholeheartedly, to the service of others. Christ dealt with selfishness not by introspection, but by giving up any preoccupation he might have had with himself, and giving himself wholeheartedly to the service of God. Christ showed how he allowed his Father to set the agenda for his life when he said to his friends, 'I don't do anything on my own account. I only do what I see the Father doing' (John 5:19). As far as Christ was concerned, 'doing the Father's will' was where it was at for him. 'I have food and drink that you don't know anything about. My food and my drink is to do the Father's will' (John

4:32,34). For Christ, doing the Father's will meant living a life of service to others. 'I have come not to be served, but to serve, and to give my life as the sacrifice I want to make in serving others' (Matthew 20:28).

I am convinced that if we want to develop a co-operative society, rather than a capitalist society—a society which really cares for people as people, not just as producers or consumers, but as people—then we must overthrow the tyranny of our own self-centredness. I remember with some embarrassment, one of my earliest attempts to deal with my own selfishness. As usual, given my flair for melodrama, my effort to deal with my selfishness was a flawed heroic affair. At the time I was sick and tired of being selfish, so I decided that I would stay inside my house, and set aside a whole month to fast and pray, until I was sure that I could emerge from my suburban cell like a butterfly from a cocoon, brilliantly and beautifully selfless. I actually followed through on my resolution, and hungrily paced around the empty rooms of my house for four long weeks, praying that every thought and every feeling I had would be self-less. But the catch was, that the more I prayed about trying to be *less* self-conscious, the *more* self-conscious I became. So I emerged at the end of the month more self-centred than when I had started!

Since that time I have discovered that the best way to deal with my selfishness, is not by trying to conquer my self in an epic struggle, but by simply trying to become more conscious of others in the midst of my daily life. I have found it very useful to start the day with a time of prayer. When I pray, I often find myself automatically going through a list of personal requests. Which is okay. It's as good a place as any to start. But it's not a good place for me to end up. So, having gone through the items on my list of the things that I'd like God to do for me, I tear it up, and toss it in the bin. Then I take a blank piece of paper and, in the quiet, I start writing down a list of things that I believe God would like me to do around the place.

Sometimes the ideas that come to mind are the obvious. But the issue for me is not whether the idea is obvious or not, but whether it is something I ought to do or not. Often it has it meant getting up early to make a cuppa for my wife and breakfast for my kids. It has meant helping get the kids off to school as well as getting ready for my own work that day. It has also meant contacting people I know in the neighbourhood that need help.

Occasionally the ideas that come to mind are not as obvious. One day I got the idea that I should visit a lonely man who lived across the street. I had tried to visit him many times before, but in vain. For some reason or another I could never seem to catch him at home—which was a shame, since I knew he'd been sick and probably needed someone to cheer him up. But what to do? I had done all that I could. So when I got the idea that I should visit the man across the street I was inclined to ignore it. I thought it would be just a waste of time. But as I was slowly but surely learning to listen to voices other than my own, I noted the Spirit's prompting, and, before I went to work, I strolled across the street to make an unscheduled visit. Lo and behold, he was home. I could hardly believe it. My neighbour was very happy that I had dropped by for a visit, and it proved to be a tonic for both of us. Just as well I didn't ignore that still small voice!

It sounds simple. And in one sense it is. It's not very complicated. But in another sense it isn't. It's very difficult for egocentric human beings, like me, not to be self-centred. I no sooner make space for God, than I take it back again. It's an ongoing struggle for me to keep God, and his agenda for my world, at the centre of my concerns. But in every situation I have ever been in, there has always been someone around, who has been able to de-centralise their ego, and encourage people around them to be self-directed but other-orientated.

At the moment much of my encouragement comes from Boyd and Sheri Ellery who live just a couple of houses down the road. Boyd and Sheri literally own next to nothing. Everything they've had, they have given away. Every day they start the day with prayer. In prayer, they empty themselves of their plans for the day. And they wait—vacant, available, accessible—ready to help anyone in need. One day Boyd will help the guy next door with his vegetable garden. Another day Sheri will help Ange and I prepare for a big party for Navi's twenty-first birthday. On other days Boyd and Sheri will help Neil and Penny care for their mother with dementia. On Wednesdays Boyd and Sheri and their three kids come to our house to pray with us, and they never pray with us without inspiring us to be a little more ready to help someone in need.

Ideas for meditation, discussion, and action

Reflect: What are some things God wants us to do for others?
Relate: How can we make sure that we do these things?
Respond: Which of these things will we start with right now?

10 Breaking Barriers of Fear

Some time back, I spent a number of weeks talking to a church about how they could become involved in their local community. Discussions had gone well. The congregation had quickly identified a range of isolated people in the community that they could get involved with. But when it came to putting their plan into operation, their enthusiasm suddenly evaporated. 'Why?' I asked them in astonishment. 'Because we are scared,' they replied. 'If we visit those people, chances are they will visit us. Then we'll never get rid of them. They'll just keep hanging around the house like a bad smell.' They wanted to get involved, but they were afraid.

Fear of the unknown. Fear of others. Fear of ourselves. Fear of success. Fear of failure. Fear of risking private space. Fear of losing personal security. Fear of fear itself. We are all full of fears. And each and every fear stands like a street corner bully, ready to take us apart if we dare to cross the line and actually get involved in the community.

Christ was no stranger to fear. When large crowds surrounded him, he knew the threat they could be to him. He had no illusions about a fickle public. John says that Christ didn't trust the crowds because he knew what was in their hearts (John 2:24–25). He knew how they could use him, and abuse him. He knew that eventually they would turn against him and would stab him in the back as soon as pat him on the shoulder. But although there were times Christ didn't trust people, there was never a time he didn't care for them. Christ looked beyond the threat and saw their need. Instead of recoiling in fear, he reached out and embraced them—even the people whom he knew would betray him.

Christ overcame his fear by developing a compassion for people that was more powerful than his concern for himself or his own safety. When confronted by a man with a sickening case of leprosy, Mark says, Christ 'was moved with compassion, reached out his hand, and literally *touched* him' (Mark 1:41). He touched a man that everyone else in his society was too scared to touch. Note, Mark says, that it was Christ's sense of compassion that compelled him to overcome his fear and impelled him to reach out his hand and touch the man that no one else would touch. The compassion that helped him overcome his fear was inspired by listening as a child to the beat of his Father's throbbing heart. He knew how much his Father was pained by the suffering of his children, and he was willing to risk his life to relieve that pain. But his compassion was not only inspired by divine passion, it was also inspired by human experience, of the needs of the people around about him.

John says Christ 'became flesh and dwelt among us' (John 1:14). Not only did he choose to live among us, he chose to live like us. Paul says, 'though he was rich, yet he became poor' (2 Corinthians 8:9). He made our poverty his own. As a pauper, he experienced the same hassles and the same hardships as everybody else. So Christ overcame much of his fear of involvement with people through prayer on the one hand, and empathy on the other. But in the end, Christ overcame his fear by being more afraid of what would happen if he *didn't* get involved, than if he *did*. For him to watch the suffering of the poor from a safe distance, and not lift a finger to help them, was a far more terrifying scenario than joining them in their struggle and sharing in their suffering. To compromise his commitment to fight for justice, was far more frightening to him than being killed for his core values. The death of his soul if he did nothing, was a much more appalling prospect than the death of his body for doing something (Matthew 10:28).

We can deal with our fear of involvement as Christ did. Many of our fears are fears of the unknown. They are based on ignorance or prejudice, rather than reality. These fears can be dispelled simply by coming to terms with the facts. For instance, more often than not, getting to know our neighbours can dispel our fear of getting involved with them. A little while ago a friend of mine wanted to get involved with a person in the community with a disability. But he was afraid of getting involved, because he felt awkward around people with disabilities. He didn't know anybody with a disability, and he didn't know how to relate to anybody with a disability. He was embarrassed to admit it, but he was actually quite scared. However, after I was able to introduce him to a neighbour with a disability, and they were able to spend some time together, he discovered to his delight that his neighbour was pretty much like him. His fear, based on ignorance, totally disappeared in the light of his discovery of their common humanity.

But not all fears are so easily dealt with. Some fears have no basis in reality, but some do. One night I was walking down the street and came across a man being attacked by a couple of hoods, who were stabbing him with the jagged shards of a broken bottle. His face was already covered in blood. And the hands he used to protect his face were already badly cut and bleeding. I thought, if someone doesn't do something soon, this chap could be cut to pieces. I looked up and down the street. But no one else was around. I knew I it was up to me to do something myself; but I must confess I was tempted just to walk on by, to pretend that I hadn't seen anything warranting my attention, let alone my intervention. I was afraid, terribly afraid, and my fear was well founded. It had a strong basis in fact. There were two men across the road trying to kill someone, and if I tried to help him, chances were that I could be killed too. After all, there were two of them, and only one of me.

They looked like street fighters, and I looked like the wimp that I was. I had no weapon, and wouldn't know how to use one even if I had one; and they had shards of sharp glass, that they wielded as wickedly as the grim reaper himself might have swung his scythe.

Fear such as this should not be dismissed, because fears based on reality act as a basic reality test for our intentions. Believe it or not, on a number of occasions, when confronted with people who wanted to kill him, even Christ decided that it was better for him to run away and fight another day than to die for nothing at all (Luke 4:29-30). And sometimes it might be better for us to run away too—the faster the better. However, this was not one of those times. This time someone's life was at stake. Christ would not have run away on this occasion, and neither, really, could I. So I wrapped the tattered rags of my makeshift courage around me, and with trembling hands, wobbly knees, and a heart ringing like an alarm bell, crossed the road to intervene in the fight.

I didn't rush over and try to crash-tackle the assailants. That only ever works in the movies. And even then it doesn't work all the time. I simply walked to within ten metres of the melée, stopped, and said from a safe distance the most inoffensive thing I could think of the time, which was 'G'day.' The antagonists immediately turned in my direction. Now I had their attention I tried to distract them from further hurting their victim. But the trick was to do it without them harming me instead. So I said to them in as friendly a tone as I could muster, 'Can I help you?' The aggressors looked at one another, then at me, and laughed. They thought it was a big bloody joke. 'Does it look like we need any help?' they asked facetiously. 'No.' I said very carefully. 'It doesn't look like *you* need any help. But, it looks like *he* might need some help. What d'you reckon?' By now they had stopped stabbing their prey, and, in answer to my question, they shrugged their shoulders, and said, 'Well *you* help him then!' And with that, they walked off, and left me to care for the mutilated man on the side of the road. He was seriously injured, but at least he was still alive. And so was I.

I've intervened in many violent situations in my life. Sometimes I've been beaten up so badly I've had to be hospitalised. One time I had to be rushed in for emergency surgery. But that was when I was younger, and intervened more aggressively, unconsciously escalating the spiral of violence in the situation. Now I'm older, I'm a little wiser. These days I am very wary about intervening. When I do, I am very careful to do it as peacefully as I possibly can. My fear doesn't usually stop me. But it does usually slow me down. Which is exactly what fear ought to do. Not stop us, but slow us down, and make us more careful about the way we go about getting involved with people.

Ideas for meditation, discussion, and action

Reflect: What's something we've been scared about, that we should do?

Relate: How can we overcome these things we are fearful of?

Respond: Which thing we have been fearful of, will we do today?

11 Breaking Barriers of Spitefulness

Most of us function according to a policy of reciprocity or retaliation: a 'tit-for-tat' approach. We are told we are to treat others just like they treat us. If they do us a good turn, then we should do them a good turn. 'You scratch my back, I'll scratch yours.' If they give us any trouble, then we have a right to give as good as we get: 'An eye for an eye, and a tooth for a tooth.' Vengeance is smart, mercy is stupid, and a smack in the mouth for someone who's crazy enough to try to insult us is nothing but pure poetic justice.

There's no bigger barrier to creative involvement in a community than the cycles of action and reaction the payback approach sets in motion. I can remember one pastor saying to me, 'Unless the people in the community cross the threshold of our sanctuary, I'm not prepared to waste my time on them.' I can remember a priest once telling me, 'We don't mind those people using our church facilities, but if they break anything we'll kick them out quick smart.' Another minister once took me aside and declared, 'We are assessing the cost-effectiveness of our community programmes. Those that have not produced enough converts over the last twelve months will have to be axed.' All these comments by clergy indicate a willingness for people in the church to get involved in the community on certain terms. And what are those terms? There must be a payback of some kind or other, and it must be positive. If there is no payback—or if the payback is negative—then they say they will withdraw their involvement. That's the way things work. It's good for good, and evil for evil.

That may sound sensible enough. But as soon as someone makes a mistake, the payback approach sets in motion vengeful cycles of action and reaction that destroy community. It is only as we break with the payback approach, and try to be *proactive,* rather than *reactive*, returning good for evil, rather than evil for evil, that we can be free to build and rebuild community, in spite of the mistakes that we make. If we are to play a constructive, rather than destructive, role in our communities, we cannot afford to be reactionary conservatives—treating others as they treat us; we need to be proactive revolutionaries—treating others like we would like to be treated ourselves. Christ said, 'Do unto others as you would like them to do to you' (Luke 6:31). He said, 'Love your neighbour as you love yourself' (Luke 10:27). 'Not only your friends, but also your enemies' (Luke 6:27). He said, 'Love those who hate you. Bless those who curse you. Pray for those who torment you' (Matthew 5:44). He said, 'Do not just do good to people who do good to you; do good to all people—regardless of what they do, or do not do, to you' (Luke 6: 32-35). Our broken communities can never be rebuilt unless we develop a 'good' approach to people, which does not depend on receiving 'good' in return for our investment, and is not diminished by having evil returned for good. Thus Christ urged his disciples to become good like God, 'who causes the sun to shine on the saints—and sinners—alike' (Matthew 5:45).

To do evil for good is demonic. To do evil for evil is human. To do good for evil is divine. So in order for us to be able to do good for evil, we must exorcise our demonic tendency to vent our frustration; transcend our normal human reaction to want to avenge any violation against us; and call on God for divine inspiration, to help us renounce evil, and channel the energy released by outrage—when evil is done to us, or those we care for—into good, honest, constructive acts of tough but tender lovingkindness.

Christ was well aware of the difficulty of doing good for evil. He knew it would mean giving ourselves to those who would not only be ungrateful for our help, but also take advantage of us. So he counselled us to 'give without expecting anything good being given back in return' (Luke 6:35). He knew it could mean we would be used, and abused; but he expected us to be willing to suffer violence, rather than inflict violence. He advocated for us to be forgiving towards people, no matter how many times they might rip us off. He said, 'If your brother, or sister, rips you off seven times a day, and seven times a day comes back to you, and says that he, or she, is sorry—forgive them' (Luke 17:4). Instead of returning 'tit-for-tat', he wanted us to turn the other cheek. 'If anyone hits you on the cheek', he said, 'turn the other' (Matthew 5:39). It is the only way that any of us will ever be able to do good for evil.

Christ says *we must give, forgive, and suffer, till we have exhausted our reserves; then ask God for the strength to give, forgive, and suffer some more.* We are to give—as long as it meets someone's need. We are to forgive—as long as it sets someone free. We are to suffer—as long as our suffering creates the chance for a human being to be born again. We have reached the limits of the usefulness of our giving, forgiving, and suffering, only when our giving and forgiving makes us irritable, our suffering makes us resentful, or our generosity makes others incorrigible. If we become irritable or resentful, Christ said we must pray for grace to extend our capacity to give and forgive, in spite of how much we may have to suffer (Luke 6:32–36). However, if the people we are relating to are incorrigible in their mistreatment of us, Christ said we should confront them face to face, and work the issue out with them (Matthew 18:17). He says that if it works out, we should continue to hang in there with them, and help them in any way we can; but if it doesn't, we should let the matter rest, and move on either physically, or psychologically, or both (Matthew 10:23). *Christ calls us to be willing to lay down our lives gladly to help people; but he doesn't expect us to be locked into violent and abusive relationships that don't help anyone at all.*

Ange and I are painfully aware of the need to be proactive rather than reactive. We constantly monitor our responses to situations so we are aware of our attitudes, and where they are wrong, we put them right. One morning I awoke to find Ange talking to herself in the mirror. She was just sitting there, muttering to herself. I thought she'd cracked up. She had been under an enormous amount of pressure over the past few months, trying to help a woman who was going through a tough time. She had worked with the woman day and night, and she was totally exhausted. But the woman had begun to make real progress, which everyone attributed to the support Ange had given her. Everyone, that is, except the woman herself. She gave Ange no credit at all. In fact she regularly abused Ange in public, telling everyone in the neighbourhood that Ange had said she was going to help, but hadn't done anywhere near enough. So when I saw Ange talking to herself in the mirror, I thought that the pressure must have finally got to her, and that she'd had a breakdown. I rolled over a little closer to see if I could pick up what she was talking about. And I'll never forget what I heard her saying to herself. 'No matter how hateful she is to me, she can't make me hate her. I will not hate her. I am going to love her. No matter what she says. No matter what she does. No matter how long it takes. So help me God!'

Over the next year, Ange must have chanted this mantra in the mirror at least once every day: over 365 times. 'I will not hate her. I'm going to love her. No matter what she says. No matter what she does. No matter how long it takes. So help me God.' Ange made sure she stuck to her task. Eventually her love broke through the hatred, and slowly but surely she managed to develop a really good friendship out of a very bad relationship.

In our experience, doing good for evil always involves pain. Strangely enough, it is often the people who need us most, who cause us most pain. They desperately want our friendship, but they feel they need to test our sincerity. The intensity of the test usually depends on the extent of their suspicions; and the extent of their suspicions usually depends on the degree to which they have been ripped off by people they trusted in the past. Ange and I have come to accept the pain of people putting us the test as the price we need to pay to in order to prove our sincerity and our integrity.

Doing good for evil is, by definition, at the heart of all 'good' community development. It may not transform every bad relationship into a good friendship; but it is the only thing that ever has done, and the only thing that ever will.

Ideas for meditation, discussion, and action

Reflect: Who are the people that are giving us a hard time at the moment?

Relate: How could we turn things round, and begin to do good for evil?

Respond: What is one good thing that we will do for them from now on?

A Heart For Building Bridges

The days that go by become days that are gone;
　　But there's time enough yet to come.
The years have grown wings and the years have flown;
　　But my time still ambles along.

There's time to spend with the family.
　　There's time to play with kids.
There's time to visit the relatives.
　　There's time to pray for the sick.
And there's time to meet the people in the street.
　　And there's time to greet the poor.
And there's time to help a neighbour in need.
　　And there's time to give a bit more.

It seems like we're living in eternity,
　　And there's always time to spare.
It seems like we're living with the certainty,
　　That there's always time to care.

'Time To Care' from the album Wonder Come *by Dave Andrews*

12 Building Bridges to People

When we moved into our neighbourhood, we visited all the people in our immediate area. The range of reactions was amazing. Some welcomed us. But many peered through the curtains, not daring to open the door. Others opened the door, but stayed behind the security grille, relating to us through their stranger-danger safety screens.

One day I tried to greet one of these neighbours in the street. 'G'day,' I said with a smile. 'What are you?' he growled, 'an encyclopaedia salesman or something?' The reality was that most of our neighbours were very suspicious of us. They could only conceive of someone wanting to relate to them if they had something to sell. In their minds there wasn't much room for a neighbour who just wanted to pass the time of day. Sadly, it is often some of my friends at church who prove my neighbours are right to be suspicious. Religious people are notorious for not having time for their neighbours—except, of course, when it is time for their annual evangelistic programme, when, armed with the latest, greatest, you-beaut marketing techniques, people in the church psych themselves up to go out into the community, and try to sell their neighbours their particular brand of religious experience.

So how do we build bridges to span the deep chasm of suspicion which divides our society? For a start, we need to put a total ban on hit-and-run raids on our communities. No matter how well-intentioned, they only make matters worse. Then we need to set about the task of painstakingly developing an identity that makes us an integral part of our local community. It is possible to live in a local community, but not become a part of its identity. Commuters do it all the time. It is only as we identify with the 'locals' and are identified as a 'local' that the bridges of relationship can be built over the chasm of alienation.

Christ recognised the importance of this process. For thirty out of the thirty-three years of his life—ninety per cent of his time—Jesus was just the boy next door in a nondescript village called Nazareth. There, he grew, so the records say, 'in favour with God, and his neighbours', developing a credible local identity as Jesus of Nazareth. Even when he began his public life, he deliberately played down his superstar status as 'the Messiah', preferring to refer to himself as a 'Son of Man'. He wanted to remain the bloke next door, so people would not be put off by the stories that the press put out (Mark 1:25, 43–44, 8:29–30).

Unfortunately, many followers of Christ focus on the last three years of his life, and forget the first thirty years. After all, they say, it was only in the last three years that he *did* anything. He didn't do anything, they say, in the first thirty years of his life. However I would like to suggest that it was what he was doing in the first thirty years that gave him the credibility to do what he did in the last three years. During these last three years he addressed the needs of the community, but it was the first thirty—when he was taught the language, learned the culture, developed his connections, picked up the stories circulating around town, and deeply heard the people who were hurting—that gave him the right to speak about the issues that affected the community. Unlike those who have claimed to follow in his footsteps, Christ knew that without the integrity of the first thirty years, the activity in the last three years would have no credibility.

There can be no substitute for the long process of building a credible, local identity. It is the foundation for any bridges we might want to build in the community. We lay this foundation when we introduce ourselves. How we introduce ourselves lays the foundation for the bridges we want to build. By emphasising what we have in common, we can lay a strong foundation on which to build. This may seem obvious enough, but many of us don't do it. We often emphasise those things that separate us rather than those things that unite us, and consequently blow up the very bridges we are trying to build.

To identify with our neighbours, we need to introduce ourselves to them in terms of those things that we have in common with them. Thus, even though I am a member of a Baptist church, I never introduce myself to anyone as a Baptist, unless they are a Baptist. With Catholics I identify myself as a follower of Christ. With Muslims I identify myself as a fellow believer in God. With Agnostics and Atheists I usually identify myself as a seeker of truth. When I don't know where the people are coming from, in my neighbourhood I simply introduce myself as their neighbour.

But establishing a credible, local identity involves far more than introducing myself *as* a neighbour. It means *being* a neighbour. And that takes a lot of time: time I never seem to have. I always seem to be too busy to be neighbourly. I have to make the time. For me it is a constant struggle to make sure I'm not too busy to be neighbourly.

There are two types of time that we can use for building bridges in our community: *scheduled time* and *casual time*. Scheduled time involves planned meetings that are dominated by the clock and are usually formal. Casual time involves opportune moments that are orientated to the event and are usually informal. Both kinds of contact are essential for building bridges in the community. Formal contacts are a way of connecting us with representatives of groups we may not normally have access to, and may give us access to the resources of the group that they represent. Informal contacts are a way we can turn our connections into friendships which enable us to relate to one another, not in terms of our respective roles, but as real people.

Actually many formal meetings build barriers, rather than bridges. The very formality of proceedings often keeps people apart. People relate to each other on the basis of their official roles, not as long-lost relatives in the human family. If formal meetings are to build bridges between people as people, the formality of the proceedings needs to be interspersed with *informality,* so people can relate to each other authentically as brothers and sisters.

We may live in a modern society characterised by formal meetings, rather than a traditional society characterised by informal gatherings, but all of us are intuitively aware that it is in our *informal* encounters that the real business of relationship building takes place. Tragically, many of us in community organisations—including church organisations—are often so preoccupied with our programmes, that we cannot respond to opportunities to develop community, as they arise with the ebb and flow of daily life. These *kairos* moments—when people are more open than closed, and we have the opportunity to develop significant relationships with one another—often pass as quickly as they come. So it is important that we grasp these moments when they come our way, or risk losing the opportunities they present forever. In order to grasp these moments, like Christ, we must be willing to either schedule time for these events, or throw out our schedules altogether!

Kairos moments come with changes, cycles, conflicts, celebrations and chance encounters. These are the times when even the most closed people in our society are open to relationships; and they represent our best opportunity to build bridges to people in the community who would usually be suspicious of anyone approaching them.

When there is a *change* people are suspicious; but they are also curious. More often than not, at least for a little while, their curiosity usually exceeds their suspicion. And that curiosity presents us with a window of opportunity to introduce ourselves to people. The window of opportunity created by change may last a day to a week; but once a person becomes used to the change, their interest subsides, they tend to close off again, and the moment of openness passes. That is why, when I moved into my neighbourhood, I tried to visit everybody in my block in the first week. Given the suspicion of people in the inner city, as expected, people were quite wary of me. But given their curiosity, about their 'new neighbour in number eight', I got a pretty good welcome from quite a few people. Over the following weeks, those neighbours who were prepared to get to know our family spoke to those neighbours who were still a bit scared, allaying their fears of us. The relationships I established in that first week have stood me in good stead ever since.

The stages in the life *cycle* also bring with them the opportunity for new or renewed relationships, because it is at significant stages of the life cycle—birth, marriage, and death—that we are reminded of our common humanity, and we remember the similarities that transcend our differences. Everyone loves to show off a new baby. You can stop a total stranger in the street and chat with them about their toddler. When the kids first start school it's not hard to make contact with the other parents dropping off their children at the gate. And when they finally leave school, it's easy to talk to other parents about their concerns for the future of their kids. Weddings provide plenty of opportunities to get acquainted or reacquainted with people we have not had contact with. But it was a death next door that gave Ange and me the opportunity to get to know a neighbour that we hadn't been able to connect with any other way. Thea was Greek. My wife was Greek. You'd think that sharing the same culture would make them natural allies. But Thea was orthodox, and Ange was evangelical. And though that difference didn't matter to Ange, it mattered to Thea. Until her father died, and Ange and I went over to visit her, to express our sympathy, and to see if there was anything we could do to help her. At that moment somehow the differences didn't seem to matter any more. We became good friends, and we have been good friends ever since.

In community there is a phenomenon known as an 'open crowd'. It's an event in which people get together in a way that naturally draws other people in. It's the complete opposite of a closed meeting—it's an open gathering. The indicators of an 'open crowd' are colour, movement, and noise, lots of noise. If the colour and movement doesn't attract the crowd, then the noise usually will. *Conflicts* and *celebrations* are often 'open crowds'.

There is nothing like a fight at the factory, or a feud in the office, to bring people together. Ironically, conflicts can often break down the walls of alienation. Having to resolve a conflict can build bridges between people who never had to relate to each other before. For instance, in our neighbourhood there was the (in)famous 'dog poo dispute'. Some time back we had some neighbours who had a couple of huge dogs as pets. These large dogs would leap the fences and leave large deposits of dog poo in everyone's back yard. Needless to say everyone was hopping mad: hopping to avoid the dog poo, mad when they didn't quite manage to avoid it! No matter how much we complained, the owners seemed loth to take any responsibility for their charges. I can't remember exactly how we resolved the dispute— or whether we did resolve it all; all I can remember is that the dispute acted as a catalyst to draw our neighbours closer together as we struggled to find a mutually acceptable solution.

At *celebrations* people are often as happy to talk to a new person as to talk to an old friend. The multicultural fiestas that we hold in

West End each year are a fantastic opportunity to meet people from different cultures and get to appreciate each other's traditions. Religious festivals can be an ideal time to meet religious people, as long as we remember to be sensitive to the significance of particular religious festivals. Christmas is a great time to meet Christians; but it is not necessarily such a great time to get to know people from non-Christian traditions. Yom Kippur, not Easter, is the festival that will give us the best chance to get acquainted with our Jewish neighbours! Secular festivals, like national holidays, often provide a wonderful opportunity to get to know our fellow citizens. But even with national holidays there are sensitivities we need to take into account. On Australia Day, Australia's biggest national holiday, we make sure that we march with aborigines through the streets of the city, to celebrate their survival, before we have a barbecue with our neighbours in our own street. But there's no better way to get to know an Aussie than at a barbecue on Australia Day.

However, there are some people that will never respond to an invitation, no matter how many times we may try to invite them. The only way we may ever meet them is by *chance*. Some people only feel safe to relate to others if they meet them by accident. It s the only way they can be sure that they are not being set up. After all, an accidental meeting is, by definition, unpremeditated. Some time back I met a neighbour at the supermarket checkout. I'd seen him around before, but always felt awkward about approaching him, because he seemed very nervous about meeting people. But here, at the checkout, we met quite naturally. He was obviously quite at ease. So I chatted with him about the groceries. And so began a special friendship that I can't imagine could have started any other way, but by chance.

In my experience, many of these opportune moments to meet others often come at inopportune times for us. I remember one day I was rushing off to work. I'd backed my car out the driveway and across the road, ready to race up the hill and get stuck into a big pile of work that I had waiting for me on my desk. As I was about to plant the pedal to the metal, I noticed a woman from the house across the road, whom I'd never seen before. No matter how many times I'd knocked on the door of her house, she'd never ever answered. When I asked her neighbours about her, they said she had a badly hunched back, and tended to stay in her house, out of sight, venturing out only on very rare occasions. Apparently this was indeed one of those rare occasions. There she was, in her garden, tending her roses, not two metres from me. What was I to do? It was a very inconvenient time for me. But I knew it might be the only chance I would ever have to meet my reclusive neighbour. So I put on the brake, took a deep breath, turned down the window, and smiling, said, 'What beautiful roses you have!' I waited, uncertain of how she would respond, but giving her the time she needed to decide how to deal with this intrusion. After a few minutes, she looked up, and, smiling in return, said, 'Yes, they are beautiful, aren't they!' From that day on, whenever I backed my car out the driveway and across the street, ready to launch myself into orbit, Betty would be there, with her curtains opened, so she could give me a wave to start the day. We were friends.

Ideas for meditation, discussion, and action

Reflect: What do we have in common with the people in our community?

Relate: What opportunities do we have to develop relationships with them?

Respond: What time will we set aside to get together with our neighbours?

13 Building Bridges
on Relationships

By and large our society operates on superficial relationships. We ostensibly build bridges of friendship to each other, but want little or no involvement with each other. Instead we play games with each other. We all know the rules. Keep the conversation shallow, but pretend it is deep. Talk about yourself, but tune out when others talk about themselves. Use meaningful jargon, but avoid a genuine meeting of souls.

Religious people have their own variations on these games. As a friend of mine, a migrant, who has stopped going to his local church, says, 'Religious people love to play a game called "church". We all dress up, and go through our paces in the service together, and whoever looks the most religious wins. The prize for the winners is approval. No one gives a damn about really being involved in one another's lives.' After church the people go home, convinced they have had meaningful contact with one another—and shown significant concern for my friend. After all, they did pass the peace to him as part of the liturgy. But my friend feels that even though he made an effort to meet people, the encounters that he had with them were totally superficial; and the banal chatter bore no relevance to the loneliness of the single room in the boarding house to which he was consigned for the term of his natural life.

Two of the favourite games people play are the 'piety game' and the 'proselytisation game'. The object of a piety game is to convince ourselves and others of our virtue. It is characterised by judging people on the basis of petty issues. It is not concerned about meeting people at their point of need. It is about using their needs to make them look 'bad', and make us look 'good' by comparison, and prevents a genuine encounter in which we can come to terms with our common needs together. The object of the proselytisation game is to convince as many people as possible to join our cause. In the proselytisation game we treat people as faceless commodities, potential trophies for us to win—but not as people. If we meet people's needs, it is not so much to help them win, but to help us win them over. The proselytisation game may promote encounters with people, but subverts the possibility of developing relationships of mutual acceptance and respect.

Many of us, realising the destructiveness of the piety and proselytisation games, give up playing religious games. But few of us give up playing games altogether: we take up secular games instead! One of the secular games religious people play is the 'welfare game'. The object of this game is to appear as if you are involved with the needs of the community without actually getting too involved. If you play the game well, you can get a lot of credit without paying the price of costly involvement. The game begins when a group is challenged about being involved in their community. The group can't say 'no', because they would be denying the voice of their conscience. But, they find it hard to say 'yes', because of the cost. To resolve the dilemma, a committee is appointed to do the job for them. And the committee appoints a professional to do the job on their behalf.

The welfare game is played with a number of variations but the aim is always the same: to get the credit for being involved in the needs of others without actually getting involved. For example, a church may be challenged to provide support for elderly people in the community. Instead of the church members personally providing the support their elderly neighbours need to stay in their own homes, the church appoints a committee which erects an old people's home, and hires professionals to care for the senior citizens on their behalf. The church can fly their flag over the project, the committee can get accolades at the annual general meeting, and the professional can get the feeling of a job well done. But at no stage is anyone expected to take their elderly neighbours into their hearts or into their homes. The problem with the welfare game is a problem of all games: they alienate us from one another. Not only do some win and some lose; but those who win, do so at the expense of those who lose.

Christ refused to play games. He criticised people who played piety games (Matthew 23:23) and he criticised people who played proselytisation games (Matthew 23:15). He condemned those who pretended to be concerned about the welfare of others when their only concern was for themselves (Matthew 23:25). He consistently called for a *real* concern for others. His attitude was best indicated in the story he told about the Good Samaritan.

A badly beaten traveller lay bleeding by the side of the road, when a priest passed by. It was the perfect opportunity for him to practise what he preached about compassion. But the priest didn't stop to help. He was too preoccupied with his religious activities to spare the time to care for his neighbour. Then a Samaritan, whom the priest would have considered a pagan, passed by. Unlike the priest, the pagan was not so preoccupied with religious duties that he couldn't spare the time to care for his neighbour. He practised what the priest preached. He stopped and helped the traveller. In doing so the Samaritan took a grave risk—at great cost. He exposed himself to possible danger from the bandits who, for all he knew, were still lurking somewhere nearby, waiting to beat up anyone so incautious as to stop and help the traveller lying by the side of the road. As it turned out, the bandits did not rob the Samaritan. But what the bandits didn't take, the doctors did. The Samaritan went to quite considerable personal expense, to pay the bill the hospital presented him with, to care for the penniless traveller. When he had finished the story, Christ turned to the crowd, and told them to stop playing games like the priest, and start caring for people authentically like the Samaritan!

Luke 10:25-37

Christ himself developed a 'non-game-playing' way of relating to others, in which no one would win at the expense of anyone else. The relationships he promoted meant that no one won unless everyone won, and if anyone lost, then everyone shared in their loss. Christ's way of relating brought together the very people that the game-playing way kept apart, and built good bridges, on genuine relationships, to people. The story of how Christ met a Samaritan woman at the well is a classic example.

When the woman met Christ at the well, she seemed intent on only discussing mundane matters—like the water in the well. However, Christ wanted to make the conversation much more meaningful. He was happy to start with a discussion about *physical* water, but he wanted to move on to *spiritual* water and talk with the woman about the 'Water of Life', that could sustain her in her struggle. The woman tried to avoid the discussion by turning it into a religious debate. She tried to start an argument over the merits of different styles of worship in different types of groups. But Christ refused to buy into the debate. He neatly side-stepped the argument and gently moved the conversation towards a genuine meeting of their souls. The bridge that Christ built, bit by bit, developed an authentic heart-to-heart connection that carried an uninhibited exchange of heart-to-heart communication. The woman shared with him her heartache. And he took her heartache to heart.

John 4:4-26

We too need to build bridges that help us meet one another halfway, make some heart-to-heart connections, and meet one another's needs in any way that we can. I remember the day I met Pyara. An Indian who had recently arrived in Australia, Pyara was a migrant, estranged from his country, his culture, and his religion. When I met him and he discovered I could speak his language, he was thrilled. But when he, a Sikh, found out I was a Christian, he was afraid I might try to convert him. It would have been very easy for us both to play the piety game or the proselytisation game, and never develop a genuine friendship. However, much to his surprise, I embraced Pyara, not as a potential trophy, but as a fellow seeker after truth. I explained that we were both in a pagan environment and that we needed to support each other spiritually to survive. I suggested to him that we should tell one another stories from our different religious traditions. I'll never forget the stories Pyara told me. They were wonderful fables, beautifully told, that really inspired me. One was a traditional parable, about 'The Sadhu And The Dog'.

Once there was a *sadhu*—a saint—who had the reputation of being a truly compassionate soul. Well, one day the sadhu was sitting by his fireside, eating his lunch when a pariah dog came up close to him, and began sniffing round, scrounging for scraps from his lunch. But the sadhu was so engrossed in eating his enjoyable lunch of flat bread *chapatti* and clarified butter *ghee* that he didn't notice the dog at all. Then all of a sudden, before he knew it, the hungry dog leapt over the fire, lunged at his lunch, tore a fresh, hot chapatti out of his hands, and ran to the *nullah* for cover. The sadhu, realising what had happened, took off after the dog who had stolen his lunch, and ran into the dirty drain where it had fled for cover. When they saw this, the villagers scoffed at the sadhu, saying, 'We heard he was a compassionate soul; but see, the sadhu is running like a dog into the nullah to get back his chappatti!'

They were still mocking him when the sadhu returned, all covered in mud from chasing the dog in the dirty drain. 'How did you go?' the villagers asked sarcastically. 'Well', the sadhu replied. 'It was a hard chase. But I finally caught the dog who had taken my chappatti, and gave him my ghee'. When they heard what the sadhu said, the villagers were stunned into silence. So the sadhu continued. 'Chapattis are so much better with ghee', he said. 'But that rascal ran off so quickly he forgot to take the ghee. Thank God I was able to catch the hungry little fellow and give him the ghee to go with the chapatti.'

When Pyara told me this story I punched the air and cried, 'That's it Pyara, that's it! That's what connecting with one another is all about! It's going out of our way to relate to one another genuinely!'

We can start to understand some of the kinds of bridges that need to be built in our community by studying reports. Federal, state, and local government, welfare organisations and voluntary groups, universities, colleges, and libraries all carry records and research that will help us understand our communities better. National departments of surveys and statistics provide valuable information on population, health, education, economics, employment, religion and ethnicity of all local areas. We can learn valuable lessons about how to build these bridges by discussing the reported needs with leaders in our community who are reputedly trying to meet these needs. Politicians, police, practitioners, ministers, consultants, teachers, social workers and community workers can help us understand some of the complexities of trying to meet the needs in our community. But *we will never actually be able to build bridges with those in need, till we meet with people, face-to-face, as long-lost relatives in the human family.* This means getting together with people to talk about ourselves, our lives, our past hurts, our hopes for the future, the needs we perceive we have, and the way we could meet these needs together.

Some time back, the young people at our church built some bridges with the older people in our community. They decided to act when they discovered from the census data just how many older people there were in our community. The census data also indicated that many of these older people lived on their own in rented accommodation. The young people approached the older people in the church to talk about the problems they faced. They then went with Meals on Wheels to visit the older people in the community who never came to church, to discuss their needs face to face. The youngsters were horrified by the conditions that many of these people lived in, many in damp, dark, dingy dwellings. Most never went out. Few, if any, ever received visitors. All had jobs, that desperately needed doing, that they simply couldn't do themselves. So the young people decided that they would do whatever they could, to help the older people in our community. They sent out notices through Meals on Wheels to the people who were shut in and couldn't get out; and they put notices up in all the local doctors' surgeries offering their help. The notices said, 'There will be no charge for labour, but a cup of tea would be appreciated.' The young people went shopping, washed dishes, scrubbed floors, cleaned yards, and had numerous chats with the older people over innumerable cups of tea. After talking to the older people and the young people, it's hard to tell what they valued most: the jobs they got done, or the cups of tea they shared.

Ideas for meditation, discussion, and action

Reflect: Who do we know that we have a gap in our relationship with?

Relate: How could we build a bridge across that gap of alienation?

Respond: What are we prepared to do to develop a heart-to-heart connection?

14 Building Bridges through Groups

In our modern society, independence is considered a virtue, and dependence is considered a vice. Even when we talk to each other, an attitude of isolation often still exists. We may talk about our problems, but we want to solve them alone. If we seek help from others, we usually ask for advice on how we can solve our problems by ourselves. Independence is healthy. Dependence is sick. We avoid interdependence like the plague.

Even though our insistence on independence appears liberating, it is in fact debilitating. *Nothing exists in and of itself. Everything that is alive, is interdependent: and everything that is alive stays alive by being interdependent.* If we act as if we are independent, we are like branches cut from a tree, cut off from the sustenance that flows from the tree of life. Cut off from the sustenance rooted in our common human life, we cannot blossom. Not only do we lose the sense of being a part of a community, but we also lose the part of ourselves which can only be fully alive while we are part of a vibrant community. Is it any wonder therefore that we cannot solve many of our problems in society? Independence not only causes many of our problems, it also separates us from access to many of the solutions to our problems, that can only be discovered together—*interdependently*—in community.

In my experience, Christians are often as blinded by our individualism as the people in the broader community. Not only have we been shaped by the same cultural values as the rest of society, but on top of that, many of us have adopted spiritual values which reinforce our individualism, rather than diminish it. This stress on the individual over against the collective, is strongest in the pietistic churches with their over-emphasis on personal conversion, personal salvation, and personal sanctification. As a result, many Christians I know operate very individualistically indeed.

By way of contrast, Christ grew up in a close-knit Jewish village. Groups—where individuals could draw on the love, strength, and wisdom of the collective, in order to resolve their problems—were of enormous importance to him. So, given this upbringing, it is hardly surprising that Christ did most of his work with people in groups. Christ started with existing groups: from conservative groups like the traditional Hebrew synagogue in Nazareth, his home town, through to radical groups like the charismatic Messianic movement in Jordan, led by his cousin John. Christ only started his own groups when existing groups could no longer accommodate his vision, or carry out his mission. It was only after he was put out of his synagogue, and when the group led by John that he'd joined fell apart when his cousin was put in prison, that Christ decided to set up his own group.

When he did start his own groups, Christ set them up on the edge of existing groups—close enough to maintain relationships with those groups, but far enough away to create the space for a degree of experimentation not normally permitted in the existing groups. In the groups Christ established, a healthy culture of interdependence was encouraged, and people were empowered to realise their personal potential in the context of corporate support.

Ange and I have learnt the importance of doing community work through groups. We also start with existing groups. Some are informal, like our family and friends. Others are formal, like the peer support group of which I was a part, that provided help for people in our neighbourhood who were struggling with distressing psychotic experiences. Some groups are conservative, like the local evangelical church we attend. Other groups are radical, like the bunch of anarcho-syndicalists in our area, whom we join from time to time to protest together about some injustice or other.

All of these existing groups have strengths—areas in which they meet needs of others quite effectively. In those areas, we work through these existing groups. To set up a group to meet needs that these groups are already meeting would be completely ridiculous. However, existing groups also have weaknesses—areas in which they fail to meet needs of others effectively. By definition, the most needy people in our neighbourhood are those whose needs are not being met effectively, if at all, by existing groups. For their needs to be met, either established groups need to be altered, or alternative groups need to be established. Often this means setting up other groups to model the change required. These emergent groups may be just inside, or just outside, existing groups. They need to be close enough to enable ongoing relationships, but far enough away to allow experimentation with the change that is required.

Ange and I try to set up such groups on the creative edge of existing groups. For example, some time back I encouraged a congregation I was working with to disband their women's fellowship, to start a support group for single mothers under stress. At the same time Ange developed a support group to provide self-help for women who were victims of abuse and brutality. This group was established on the edge of a large congregation which already provided crisis accommodation. Developing this support group to provide self-help for women helped this congregation, already interested in women's issues, to move from short-term care to long-term commitment to women at risk.

Starting a support group can be both surprisingly easy, and infuriatingly difficult. Christ suggested it could be as easy as two or three people recognising a common concern. He suggested we begin to work out our common concerns for the neighbourhood over meals in one another's homes (Luke 10:7). However, at times, the search for people with a common concern can be extremely difficult and frustrating. Search as we may, we just can't seem to find someone whose heart beats in harmony with ours. These are times of quiet desperation, which call for quiet determination. We need to heed the advice of Christ, who said to his disciples, 'Look, and look, and keep on looking—for only then will you find what you are looking for!' (Matthew 7:7). We need to look among people we already know, who may be interested. We should talk to these people about our concerns. On the one hand, they may think we are crazy. But on the other hand, they may share our concerns. We should also look at existing groups that may be engaging in activities closely related to those we are interested in. When we find two other people, and three of us decide to work together, then a group has formed.

Starting a group can be difficult, but it is never as difficult as the task of *maintaining* the group. Power struggles are the biggest reason that groups blow up. Christ suggested that the best way to deal with power struggles was to make sure there were no bosses in a group: that everyone in the group operates, not as bosses, but as servants working for the welfare of everyone else in the group (Matthew 23:8). Of course, all groups need leadership. But Christ's idea of being a leader had nothing to do with control. For him, being a leader meant being a facilitator. He said that in support groups, 'the leader should be the servant' (Matthew 23:11): not controlling the group, but facilitating.

Understanding the development phases that all groups pass through can be helpful to facilitators. The most commonly recognised phases are *forming, storming, reforming* and *performing*. Forming is when the group first gathers around a common concern. Storming is when the group tries to find solutions to the problems. This usually involves a sequence of stormy disputes. Reforming is when these disputes are resolved and the group finds a practical way forward. Performing is the carrying through of agreed strategy. All groups pass through these phases and in any dynamic, growing group, these phases will occur over and over again. Facilitators who are aware of these phases can initiate when the group is forming; conciliate when the group is storming; consolidate when the group is reforming; and co-ordinate when the group is performing.

Groups must be developed with a lot of care if they are genuinely to help people grow. They must be open, not closed; inclusive, not exclusive; co-operative, not competitive; big enough to have a critical mass and creative mix of people, but small enough for all the people to be able to participate meaningfully; and dynamic enough for everyone in the group to be active, not passive members of the group. Because of the time and attention that groups require, it is important that we limit the number of groups we are involved in. Those of us operating in the local community in the context of a local church, probably need to restrict ourselves to involvement in just three groups: one larger group for meeting together and two smaller groups for action and reflection.

Each Monday morning from 6 to 7, for the last twenty years, I have made my way, through the twilight in winter and the sunrise in summer, to meet with a group of half-a-dozen to a dozen friends. The Monday morning meeting is a small community group made up of people from the Waiters' Union who gather together at the beginning of each week to consider what the issues are in the neighbourhood, and how our network might best be able to respond to them. After a time of discussion we decide on the actions we could take, then circulate our proposals for approval, or disapproval, through a newsletter that we distribute to all the households in the network by Monday night. This is a classic *action group*, committed to specific, concrete, immediate action—from rallying round the Aboriginal community over a suspicious death of a young person in police custody, to raising the money to buy a set of false teeth for a poor woman who wanted nothing more than to be able to flash a bright smile for her beloved on her wedding day.

Each Friday morning from 10 to 12, for the last twelve or thirteen years, I have headed out to try to find where I am supposed to meet with another group of half-a-dozen friends. The Friday morning meeting is a small cell group made up of people in the Waiters' Union who gather together at the end of each week, to contemplate the issues arising in our personal, family, and community lives, and to ponder how well we are dealing with them. We meet in a different home each week, and we often forget which home we are meeting in, so we often get lost trying to find our meeting venue—me more than most. In fact, I can remember one day going round to everyone's house, looking in vain for where the group was supposed to meet, only to arrive back home and find everyone waiting for me on the front steps of my own house. We often say to one another that the difficulty that we have in getting to the group is typical of the difficulty we have in getting to the truth that the group is meant to help us get to. However, over the years, it has got a whole lot easier. These days, when we get together we very comfortably, very quickly, settle down to a depth of authenticity and honesty in our conversation. This is a classic *reflection group*, committed to real, vulnerable, meaningful reflection. We talk, we listen, and give and receive feedback; we laugh, we cry, and give and receive affirmation; we share pots of tea, boxes of tissues, and lots of hugs.

Each Sunday night at 6:30, for the last ten years, Ange and I have met with a large bunch of up to 100 people from all over our neighbourhood, in the basement of the rather serendipitously named St. Andrew's Church. The Sunday night gathering includes many people from the Waiters' Union, but includes a lot more people from the neighbourhood than are a part of our little network. It is essentially a gathering of local people, many of whom are physically, intellectually, and/or psychiatrically challenged, and live in extraordinarily difficult social, economic, and political, life-controlling circumstances—who gather to celebrate their faith, and their life, together.

One of the locals who you would meet if you came along, is Kay Irwin. Kay goes out of her way to greet everyone who comes through the door at St. Andrew's. Her first words are, 'Hi. My name is Kay. I do dialysis.' Kay has a life-threatening kidney complaint. She has waited for a kidney transplant for years. So, three times a week, Kay has to go to the local hospital to 'do dialysis.' For her, it's a matter of life and death. But even though Kay's life has to revolve around dialysis, Kay does dialysis in style. She is up front about her struggle. She wears the scars on her arms as badges of honour. She challenges people to join her in hospital while she is doing dialysis, 'if you've got the guts.' Somehow she transforms her struggle into a sacrament for others. She sells raffle tickets to raise money for kidney research. And she draws funny cartoons to give her fellow-sufferers a bit of a belly laugh for a change. Kay Irwin and the motley crew at St. Andrew's on Sunday night are an atypical, but archetypal, *congregational group*, that help us live our lives to the full.

Ideas for meditation, discussion, and action

Reflect: What are the existing groups in our community?

Relate: Where is there need for emerging groups to start ?

Respond: What will we do to support existing and emerging groups?

15 Building Bridges for Cooperation

It is one thing to get people to cooperate with one another in a group; quite another to get the group to cooperate with other groups. Miscommunication, suspicion and competition ensure that most groups move in their own circles and keep a safe distance from one another. One might hope that the church, which preaches reconciliation, might be an exception. But experience shows the opposite is often the case.

A few years back, a coalition of local churches sponsored a Christmas celebration. It was a combined, ecumenical, inter-denominational, cross-cultural, multi-lingual celebration of the coming of Christ, held in the street right in the middle of our neighbourhood. Hundreds of people showed up, thoroughly enjoying the candlelight service, which was presented in the manifold colours of the multiple religious traditions represented. All the way through, from the Greek kids' chorus, to the Anglican parish choir, the music was mesmerising; and in the end, the Tongans blew everybody away with the beauty of their harmonies.

A week later, another church, which had boycotted the combined event, put on an event of their own—and it was a flop, a big flop. Without the contributions of the other groups the programme they put on was pretty monochrome, and monotonous. Hardly anyone turned up, and even the few people that the organisers brought with them, drifted away as quickly as they could, quietly into the night. No-one wanted to be there—it was embarrassing. No doubt this church rationalised its disastrous decision not to cooperate with the others.

Christ encouraged everyone to cooperate with everyone else, regardless of the group they belonged to. He even encouraged the orthodox to support activities promoted by heretics, as long as those activities were characterised by a concern for love and justice. Once a religious academic asked Jesus for an authoritative definition of a neighbour. In response, Christ told the Good Samaritan story that we mentioned earlier. A man, battered by robbers, and left to die on the roadside, was ignored not only by a priest but also by a Levite, representatives of the religious establishment. He was helped by a Samaritan, a man regarded by the orthodox religious establishment as a heretic. Christ then instructed the religious academic to get beyond being religious and start doing some good, like the Samaritan.

The idea of a 'good' Samaritan was repulsive to the religious academic. For Jews, the only good Samaritan was a dead Samaritan. Christ's instruction to the Jew to join the Samaritan in doing good was equivalent to his telling a Christian to work with a Muslim for the good of the community. A horrifying thought for some evangelicals, who find it difficult to conceive of working ecumenically with other Christians, let alone non-Christians! But Christ made no apologies for stressing the importance of working together as neighbours: not just with our friends, but even with those that we consider to be our enemies.

When Christ sent his disciples out to do community work, he suggested they find others they could work with. He said nothing to the disciples about checking out their religious credentials. There were just two qualities Christ said his disciples should look for in the people they wanted to work with. They needed to be peaceful and hospitable—in other words, cooperative (Luke 9:5–6). When the religious leaders of Christ's day criticised him for associating with people whose religious beliefs were dubious, Christ simply replied that he had come, not to call the religious, but to call the irreligious to the challenge of doing God's work in the community (Matthew 9:13). However, even Christ's own disciples had problems in relating to people in other groups the way Christ wanted them to. One day they stopped a man doing a good job in 'their' locality—because, they said, he did not belong to their group. Christ was appalled at their narrow-mindedness, and reprimanded them all for their short-sightedness. 'Don't stop him,' Christ instructed them, 'because whether they belong to your group or not, whoever is not against you, is for you' (Luke 9:50). For Christ, the possibility of cooperating with people with differing points of view, was not a prospect to withdraw from in horror, but an opportunity to relate to a wide range of people, that should be embraced wholeheartedly.

Ange and I have tried to follow Christ's example in this regard, by drawing together groups in the locality who are willing to work together for the welfare of the community. We have consistently tried to develop cooperation between various cliques in our congregation, and between the various congregations in our neighbourhood, by calling people together to consider common concerns. I can remember in the early days, when we were just getting started, that we talked to Ange's family about inviting a wide range of people interested in the community to come to a meeting at their house. Ange's parents' house had a huge, spacious room that was perfect for the rather large gathering that we had in mind. As people entered, we encouraged them to put a pin in a large photographic map that we had hung on the wall to indicate where they lived. As each person sat down, we encouraged them to share with the group about the concerns they had for the locality. After everyone had had a chance to share, the large group then broke into small groups, to discuss their concerns in more detail, and then to pray for one another. That such a meeting actually happened in our area was a minor miracle, as those who were invited came from a range of groups in our neighbourhood who have been very hostile to one another over the years. There were the usual suspects—Protestants and Catholics, charismatics and conservatives, evangelicals and Orthodox—all in one room at the same time. But instead of the meeting degenerating into a big, free-for-all, theological brawl, it was the beginning of a growing spirit of fellowship that made future cooperation much more feasible. As a result of that meeting, people from the local Uniting, Catholic, Episcopal, Orthodox, Evangelical, and—would you believe it?—even the traditionally separatist Baptist Church, met together every Friday, without fail, for years, to explore ways of working cooperatively together in West End.

It is possible to develop very substantive levels of cooperation between churches and other groups in the community. Churches can start by *allowing their premises to be used by other groups.* For example, St. Francis, one of the Catholic churches in our area, has allowed its premises to be used as an alternative school for local Aboriginal children. Both sides have benefited from this arrangement. The Aboriginal community got to use a facility which was otherwise over-protected and under-utilised, but very much needed; and the church got the opportunity to get to know the Aboriginal community, as no other church in the neighbourhood had ever done.

But it is possible for churches to allow their premises to be used by other groups, yet still have virtually no contact with the group at all—except when it comes time to collect the rent or pay for damages. Allowing our premises to be used by others may be the place for us to start to cooperate with other groups; but it should never stop there. George Lovell, a British Christian community development consultant, insists that we need to be willing to move on from just sharing property, to putting our time, our energy, our expertise, and our whole congregational infrastructure at the service of other groups.

- We can *help administer a programme with an already established community association which needs support*. For instance, one of our local churches helps to run a Meals on Wheels group in West End, which distributes healthy mid-day meals at minimal cost to frail, elderly people in our community. Besides offering its premises as a base for Meals on Wheels, a number of people in the congregation are personally involved in the day-to-day operations of the organisation, from preparing the meals, to providing the wheels.
- We can *help initiate a local community association to provide a needed service*. For instance, one of our local churches has set up 'Family Care Services' which provides assistance for families needing support, through a local community centre they established. The centre provides a space where people can just drop in; but it also provides a base for running playgroups, sharing information resources, running educational courses, offering counselling services and organising community development activities. The church not only originally initiated the setting up of Family Care Services, but has also continued to participate in the provision of the services by being involved in the management committee.
- We can *help personalise services of otherwise impersonal service organisations*. For instance, one of our local churches came to realise that many people in the parish who were entitled to

claim social security benefits were afraid to do so, because they found the hoops that they were expected to jump through in order to get welfare were both daunting and demeaning. So the church decided to encourage members of the congregation to get alongside these people and accompany them on their visit to their local welfare office. The fact that only four or five people out of a congregation of forty to fifty had jobs, meant that the church had lots of people with lots of experience to provide this personal service—and they did it with a vengeance!

- We can *help advocate for vulnerable people in situations of severe disadvantage*. For instance, one of our local churches monitors the accommodation problems of particularly vulnerable groups of people in our neighbourhood. When there is a complaint, members of the congregation investigate the matter, and where necessary make vigorous representations to landlords on behalf of vexed tenants. They even managed to secure a successful settlement in the notorious 'potty' case, in which a recently released psychiatric patient was threatened with eviction and an immediate return to the psychiatric facility that he had just left, due to his accidentally knocking over a potty in his flat, the urine seeping through the floor—which was the landlord's ceiling—and dripping onto the head of the unhappy landlord below. How anybody could have settled that dispute happily, I'll never know, but they did. The potty was evicted. But the tenant got to stay, on condition he went to the toilet in future!

Ideas for meditation, discussion, and action

Reflect: What other groups are we aware of in our area?
Relate: How do these groups actually relate to each other?
Respond: How can we encourage better cooperation with one
another?

A Heart for Bringing Growth and Change

I've seen the light in your eyes.
I've felt the fire in your bones.
I know the heart of your desire.
The work of care is never done.
There's a hope deep inside us
Of a beauty around the bend.
When we will all live with justice.
And the agony of this age will end.
I've heard the trouble you've been thru'.
I've felt the blows that you've borne.
I know your struggle to be true.
The work of prayer is never done.

We hope for nothin' less than
Good faith and righteousness,
True love and tenderness,
Real peace and happiness.
We hope for nothin' less.
Hope for nothin' less.
We hope for nothin'—nothin' less.

'Nothin' Less' from the album Wonder Come *by Dave Andrews*

16 Bringing About Personal Hope

If we want to try to facilitate transformation in our community, then sooner or later we are sure to be confronted by the hopelessness that completely incapacitates most people in most communities. I teach courses on transformation in many communities. At first glance, most of the people who come to these courses seem hopeful enough; but when we begin to talk about the possibility of individual and collective transformation, it doesn't take very long for the discussions to bog down in despair, and those who seem to know the most about themselves and their society seem to be those most stuck in despair.

Without hope, there is no motivation for growth or change. It doesn't matter how many courses people go to, how many skills they acquire, how many certificates they accumulate. So it is absolutely crucial that for any personal growth or social change to occur, people can experience hope in the midst of their hopelessness. But how? How do you impart hope to the woman contemplating suicide because the man she loves is having an affair with a younger woman? How do you impart hope to a man who as a child was abused by his father and now finds himself doing the same to his own children? How do you impart hope to grieving parents whose only son has been killed by a runaway truck? How do you impart hope to a whole community of people whose homes are to be demolished to make way for a freeway?

Believe it or not, Christ found *prayer* to be the most effective process that he could use to introduce hope into hopeless situations.

One day Christ got an urgent message from two close friends, Mary and Martha. Their brother Lazarus was dying. By the time Christ made the long journey to their village, the situation was hopeless. Lazarus was dead. In fact, Christ had even missed the funeral and Lazarus had already been laid to rest in a tomb.

Christ was overcome with grief. He wept openly, grieving with Mary and Martha. Going to the graveyard with them, he began to pray out loud. He deliberately prayed out loud so he could give voice to Mary and Martha's inner anguish, and in so doing, remind them that God was grieving with them. As he prayed, the family gradually became aware that no matter how hopeless the situation was, there was still hope. There was still hope because even in the midst of the hopelessness of death, a source of life existed that had the power to bring life out of death. And Christ brought life out of death when he walked over to the crypt, called for his friend to come out of the tomb, and brother Lazarus rose from the grave and strode towards his sisters, Martha and Mary.

John 11:17-44

Two very important principles can be found in this story. First, *Christ entered into his friends' hopelessness.* He did not laugh at their tears or analyse their grief. Instead he wept with them, fully embracing their grief. He did not try to promote hope until after he had fully partaken of their hopelessness. It is my conviction that prayers for hope are only meaningful to the degree that we have entered into the person's experience of hopelessness. It is only then that we can give voice faithfully to their cry to God and remind them that God will give heed to their cry.

Second, *the hope that Jesus promoted through prayer was not a fantasy experience* that deluded Mary and Martha into believing they were better off than they really were. Instead, it was a faith experience in which the painful facts of their situation were miraculously transformed, bringing them face to face again with Lazarus, whom they had believed had been lost forever. I am convinced that prayers for hope are only liberating to the extent that they are prayers of *faith* rather than prayers of fantasy. Fantasy is a fixation on a particular outcome of the future which may or may not happen. But faith is a confidence in the possibility that either our situation can change, or that we can change enough to cope with the situation as it is.

This does not mean that faith is unimaginative: quite the contrary. Prayers of faith involve encouraging people to imagine either their painful reality being totally transformed, or alternatively, the pain remaining, and themselves being transformed through the pain. Faith looks into the face of reality. Fantasy ignores it. Christ would have entered the realm of fantasy if he had encouraged Mary and Martha to imagine Lazarus rising and never having to die again. Instead, he imparted faith that imagined life coming out of death but accepted death as part of the process. Therefore prayers of hope are only liberating to the extent that they face the facts, yet allow for the facts to be transformed by God.

Like most people, I have not seen too many people come back from the dead. But I have encountered some of the greatest comebacks since Lazarus. I have often witnessed hope live again in communities where hope had died. Some time back a woman called Madie talked to me about the hopelessness that many people she knew felt as they struggled for authentic transformation. I wondered if she was reflecting her own sense of hopelessness, but did not raise the issue. A few days later Madie called on the phone. She was desperate. I dropped everything, went and picked her up and brought her home. When Madie arrived at our place, she found that she couldn't contain the pain any more, and her sense of hopelessness simply exploded all over the kitchen. She wept like a soul tortured in hell, who could endure her hell no longer. Ange and I embraced Madie as she wept over the years of accumulated brutality that she had suffered at the hands of an abusive husband. We wept together, then prayed, voicing her pain to God. There, at the kitchen table, Madie began to breathe out the hurt and breathe in the healing.

We gave Madie a bed for the night, but we didn't get much sleep. Every time Madie drifted off to sleep she would relive the torment in her dreams and wake up screaming. She would leap out of bed and pace the floor seeking peace. By morning we were all exhausted. For years Madie had borne this pain alone, believing that no-one would understand. Even if they could understand, they could never share the pain. And even if they could share the pain, how could they ever help her rise from the depths of despair? But now she had spoken of her pain. We had provided the time and space for the pain deep inside her to surface in our presence. We had tried to understand and share her pain, even if that understanding and sharing was incomplete. Through prayer, Madie began to be able to face her pain without so much despair, believing that there might perhaps be a life beyond the death of all her hopes. And in the courage and strength that hope always imparts, Madie began the difficult task of putting the pieces of her shattered life back together again, bit by bit.

Not everybody is ready to pray like Madie. People who are cynical may find the whole business about prayer a bit spooky and a bit scary. I always ask permission to pray with people. If and only if they give me their permission, do I pray with them; and then I try to do it as sensitively as I possibly can. Sometimes I ask them to pray with me, using their imagination to sensitise themselves to possibilities that they may have never considered. In my experience, most people, even those who say they don't believe in prayer, are open to my praying for them, if I voice their cry faithfully, without patronising them or preaching at them, but praying with sensitivity, empathy and respect. Although these people often feel awkward to begin with, many actually feel in the end that their cry has been heard and find new hope in the midst of hopelessness.

When praying with people, I pray with confidence: not that my wishes, or the wishes of the person will be fulfilled, but that the facts of their situation will be miraculously transformed by God, bringing the person face to face again with a life they thought was lost forever, when someone, or something, died. I have found that it is not only important to experience the person's hopelessness as you pray; it is also important to experience an infusion of hope on behalf of the person. More often than not, the person we are praying for will experience the same infusion of hope. It is then, and only then, that we can struggle with the person in helping them to put the pieces back together again.

It is more than ten years since Ange and I prayed with Madie at our table in the kitchen at our house in Highgate Hill. Since that time, Madie has continued to deal with her trauma, and the issues of that it raised for her, in the light of the hope that she experiences in prayer. She often says, 'Prayer doesn't make it painless, but it does make it possible for us to deal with our pain.' In working through her own issues Madie has been able to find a way of helping other people work with their issues. So Madie is now a fully qualified social worker, who specialises in difficult cases, helping people cope with everything from frightful cruelty through to horrifying cancer.

It is her capacity to help people face the very worst that life can throw at them, that is the reason that we asked Madie to be the supervisor of the joint household that we live in on the main street of West End. The joint household is a shared space devoted to helping people develop an everyday spirituality that relates to the struggles of ordinary, everyday life. And when Ange and I decided to move into the joint household with our daughter Navi and her friend Olivia, the best person we could think of, to help us help people face the very worst that life can throw at them, was Madie Anlezark.

Ideas for meditation, discussion, and action

Reflect: What hopelessness do we encounter in our community?

Relate: How can we help bring some hope into the hopelessness?

Respond: Who will we pray with, to breathe life into hope which has died?

17 Bringing About Political Empowerment

Hope alone cannot bring transformation. Hope is a fragile quality that is quickly destroyed by any feelings of powerlessness. Unless our feelings of powerlessness are dealt with, the hope infused today will be gone tomorrow. I think most of us are paralysed to some extent by a sense of powerlessness. Ironically, it is those of us who have tried hardest to transform the community who feel the most powerless. We know only too well how the system is stacked against anyone who wants to work for transformation. So if we are going to promote personal growth or social change, it is crucial for us to deal with our underlying sense of powerlessness. Hand in hand with hope must come empowerment.

Christ understood the causes of disempowerment: the self-doubt that debilitates us, the social indifference that breaks us, the traditional obligations that bind us, the political subjection that shackles us body and soul to the *status quo*. However, Christ not only discerned the causes of disempowerment, he also indicated the sources of empowerment that could dispel the despair and inspire people with the hope that they could make their dreams come true. Christ saw power as the ability to control ourselves, and empowerment as the process of enabling one another, individually and collectively, to exercise greater control over our lives.

Most times empowerment happens gradually, almost imperceptibly, over a long time. But sometimes it happens dramatically, in an instant.

An example of dramatic empowerment was Christ's encounter with a man with a withered hand, whom he met one sabbath at the synagogue. To this man, his withered hand represented total powerlessness. Not only was it a frustrating physical handicap, it was a social handicap. According to the religious rituals of his time, his withered arm barred him from participating fully in the temple rites of his own religion. And because it was his right hand that was crippled, he would have to use his left hand for business as well as ablutions. According to the cultural traditions of the time, this man could never participate freely in the life of the town in which he lived. For him the withered hand was a handicap that not only debilitated him physically, but also spiritually, culturally, economically, and politically.

When he saw the man at the back of the synagogue, Christ called him forward and gently encouraged him to do what he had always wanted to do, but had been powerless to do—stretch out his hand. According to Luke, who wrote the account of the incident, the man obeyed and his hand was restored.

Luke 6:6–10

In describing the incident, Luke uses an interesting turn of phrase which emphasises the fact that the restoration of the man's arm did not take place before but *after* he stretched out his hand. *It was in the process of doing what the man knew he couldn't do that he was empowered.*

I have witnessed similar dramatic instances of people being empowered. I remember once being at a neighbourhood party when a new neighbour came to the door. The newcomer was so paranoid about meeting new people, that he stood at the door, too scared to enter. He was totally paralysed by his apprehension, and my brother-in-law, Bulla, noticed him hanging back, hesitating, unsure as to whether he should be coming or going. Bulla slowly made his way round the room until he found himself standing right next to the stranger. Bulla, normally an ebullient character, eased back on the volume of his legendary energy levels, so as to be able to approach the frightened young man without freaking him out, and began to engage him quietly in conversation. With each kind word he heard from Bulla you could see the young man grow in confidence: his back straightened, his shoulders adjusted, his neck strengthened, and his head lifted to look Bulla in the eye. Bulla returned his gaze, then putting his arm around his new found friend, turned him round to face the gathered throng. Thus Bulla enabled a frightened young man to face his fears—and join the party.

Most instances of empowerment are not instantaneous. But whether the process is short and immediate or long and tedious, the essence of empowerment entails the renunciation of lies and the practice of truth. Christ insisted that it is lies that bind us and truth that liberates us. It is the lies we believe about ourselves that disempower us and stop us from growing and changing. Conversely, it is the truth about ourselves that explodes our sense of powerlessness and sets us free to grow and change. As Christ said, 'You will know the truth and the truth will set you free' (John 8:32).

Encouraging people to renounce lies and embrace truth about themselves can be difficult and frustrating. It certainly was for Christ. But Christ persisted in the process of empowering disempowered people, regardless of how arduous the process might be. To those debilitated by self-doubt, who looked at Christ as an example of what they would like to be but thought they never could be, he said, 'You know, anything I can do, you can do better' (John 14:12). To those debilitated by social indifference, who believed they could never make any difference, because nothing ever changes, he said, 'Stop cursing the darkness. You are the light of the world. If you do justice, you will shine like the sun' (Matthew 5:14 & 13:43). And to those debilitated by their obligations to tradition or their subjection to the *status quo,* who believed Christ was right, but that it was wrong to buck the system, he said, 'Forget about the system. Let the dead bury their dead. You must be prepared to die for your beliefs. If you try to preserve your life, you will waste it. But if you waste your life for me, and my revolutionary movement of love and justice, you will preserve the spirit that makes life worth living' (Matthew 8:22, 10:34–39).

If we seek to be involved in empowering the disempowered, we need to encourage them to renounce the lies that promote counterproductive and self-destructive reactions, and embrace the truth that will enable them to act in a responsible, self-disciplined manner that allows them to take control over their own individual and collective lives.

Some time back, Ange and a few of her friends got involved with a group of people in our community who felt totally powerless. Some had brain tumours. Others had brain damage from strokes. Some were developmentally handicapped. Others suffered from a psychiatric disability of some kind or other. All of them had been institutionalised; all of them felt that they could not really function properly in the community without the presence of ongoing support from institutionalised services in their lives. As Ange and her friends got to know these people, they became increasingly aware of the powerlessness these people felt, and they gradually began to feel some of that powerlessness themselves. They were tempted to believe only professionals could help these people. How on earth could they help? What could they as amateurs do, that the professionals had not already done? Ange and her friends wanted to find a way to do something to help their new-found friends, but they were tempted to believe that, because they were amateurs, there was nothing they could do. In order to be able to do anything, Ange and her friends found that they needed to consciously renounce the lie that amateurs cannot help, only professionals can; and consciously embrace the truth—that's as old as the hills—that friends can help one another too. In the process, they discovered that there is one thing that a friend can do, that a professional-as-a-professional can never do for a client-as-a-client, and that is to relate to them in an unpaid capacity, as a friend.

The greatest challenge for Ange and her friends was to find ways to empower people who were totally and thoroughly disempowered as a result of their institutionalisation. They made a number of choices about their approach that proved to be quite crucial.

- They decided not to come across in an overpowering manner that might only serve to further disempower people. They were determined to relate to each person as an individual, not as a member of an institution, so that their personal identity was strengthened over against the corporate institutions that regulated so much of their lives.
- They committed themselves to help the people explore their views about life they were living, and the life they wanted to live, in order to raise their consciousness of themselves as potent human beings.
- They sought to help the people develop their capacity for growth and change by helping them realise the significance of the insights, knowledge, and skills that they already had.
- They eagerly confirmed the truth and gently confronted the lies that emerged in their conversations with people; encouraging the people to renounce their delusions, embrace their reality, and take responsibility for their own development.

- Wherever possible, Ange and her friends suggested to people that they work together on projects as a group, rather than as individuals, so as to experience their power as part of a collective.

It would be lovely to say that as a consequence of Ange and her friends' involvement, none of these people feel powerless any more. But unfortunately that is not true. Many of them feel as powerless as they did before Ange and her friends befriended them. But because Ange and her friends have treated them with respect, the people have become more respectful of themselves. Because Ange and her friends related to them as people in their own right, many of these people have begun to feel more of their own importance as people. They have begun to explore aspects of themselves they had not come to terms with before, particularly those parts of themselves which they had felt guilty about, and which had caused others to reject them.

Many have actually managed to make significant progress. A few have started to find more solace in themselves than they found in the bottom of a bottle. Some have begun to develop new living skills in preparation for moving into independent living situations in the community. Many have established interdependent relationships with people in the community characterised by mutual regard and enjoyment. A few have started to realise some of their incredible potential to make a vital contribution to the life of the community through paid and unpaid work. Some have even begun to actively participate in critical reviews of government policy with regard to health programmes that have impacted adversely upon their lives. As they have renounced the lies that had left them powerless, they have been able to embrace the truth that they have the power in their own hands, to control their own individual and collective lives.

I have watched three young men, whom everybody considered nobodies, actually turn their world around. Barry, Gary and Dan were unemployed young men, with long histories of serious psychiatric disorders, who wanted to work with other unemployed young people in their neighbourhood. They were highly motivated, but their ideas seemed to be hopelessly unrealistic. Barry, Gary, and Dan had none of the qualities that would normally be required of a group putting their hands up to organise an employment project. They had no funding, no skills, and no staff; and they were quite fragile, often unreliable, and very unpredictable. The only thing they had going for them, apart from their desire to do something with the unemployed, was their experience of being unemployed themselves. Now that might be great for empathising with the unemployed, but it's not so great for developing an employment project, which I reckon is one of the hardest tasks in community work, and all the harder if the project is targeted, as theirs was, at providing employment for people in extreme poverty who were chronically ill and had no obviously marketable skills.

Barry, Gary, and Dan spent time a lot of time together exploring their options. They experimented with different possibilities—and failed, and failed, and failed again. But they refused to give up. One day, when they were brainstorming, out of the blue Barry came up with the idea of recycling garbage. Gary and Dan thought it was a great idea. As it so happened, it turned out to be the right idea at the right time. They set up a garbage recycling cooperative, and got every available body to work, recycling garbage. Now anyone who has anything to do with co-ops knows that they can be fraught with incredible difficulties. And this co-op was no exception. It was fraught with every difficulty imaginable—from nightly rivalry to daylight robbery—and, as a result, it ended up a failure. But unlike some of their other ventures, the co-op was not an absolute disaster.

Through the co-op, Barry, Gary, and Dan had succeeded in helping people learn to generate a basic income for themselves, not through a handout, but through the work of their hands, and consequently to develop their confidence in their ability to gain and maintain a greater degree of individual and collective control over their own lives.

Ideas for meditation, discussion, and action

Reflect: What powerlessness do we encounter in our community?

Relate: What is the truth that can empower disempowered people?

Respond: How can we help people gain greater control over their lives?

18 Bringing About Problem Resolution

Even after hope has been infused and people feel empowered to take control of their own lives, there is the nitty-gritty business of getting down to resolving problems. A mechanical problem can be solved once and for all. But problems in human relationships are never solved once and for all: they must be resolved over and over again by the people involved. A community that is transformed is not one without problems; it is one which has developed a process for resolving problems. In fact, a community is transformed only to the degree that everybody in the community can participate freely and fairly in resolving their problems together. The essence of transformation is in creative problem resolution.

It is instructive to look at the role Christ played in settling disputes. Even though Christ was unafraid to state his opinion publicly, when it came to stating his views on how a particular dispute should be settled, he often refused. When people asked him a question about a situation, that projected the responsibility of answering the question away from themselves and onto him, Christ usually refused to answer. Christ wanted people to own their own predicament, accept the responsibility for their own problems, and accept the responsibility of resolving them. One day two brothers came to Christ to settle a dispute that they were having over the division of their family property. Christ, in his typical style, answered the question with a question: 'Man, who made me a judge over you?' (Luke 12:14) Christ used this technique of questioning the questioner to make people answerable to themselves. It was often in the answering of a question that the person would be forced to take responsibility for solving their own problem.

While Christ refused to allow people to project the responsibility for solving their problems onto him, he also stated quite clearly that they shouldn't project the responsibility onto anyone else either—particularly the experts. He actually warned people to 'beware of experts' (Luke 20:46). He told people that they themselves were the experts on their own problems. Instinctively they knew the answers. 'Why don't you judge for yourself what is right?' (Luke 12:57) Christ knew that nobody, no matter how expert they might be, could solve someone else's problems for them. Ultimately everyone has to solve their own problems. That is why Christ insisted that if you have a problem with someone, you must deal with it 'between you and him or her alone' (Matthew 18:15).

However Christ also recognised that many of us need someone to help us in our struggle to solve our problems. The difference is that this person must act as a *helper*, not an expert. They are there to help us solve the problem, not to solve it for us. Christ said about problem solving, 'If someone wrongs you, go and show them their fault, between you and them alone. But if they will not listen to you, take one or two others with you' (Matthew 18:16). The role of these 'one or two others' was not to take sides or give advice. They were there to help clarify the situation by enabling the various parties involved to listen to each other and talk about possible solutions. Christ called these third-party helpers 'witnesses'. Their job was to bring the truth to light by faithfully declaring the facts as they saw them emerging from the murky shadows of the dispute. And it was in this role of witness, rather than judge, that Christ himself preferred to operate.

One day Christ was teaching, when a whole crowd of noisy people arrived dragging a woman who had been caught red-handed having an affair. They wanted Christ to pass judgment on her. According to Jewish law, if this woman was an adulterer, she was meant to be executed, and traditionally adulterers were executed by stoning.

Christ had gone on public record as being totally opposed to affairs. As a matter of fact, Christ had gone much further than the law, and claimed that if anyone even entertained the idea of having an affair with someone that they weren't married to, they were already an 'adulterer' in their hearts. So when the woman was caught red-handed, having an affair, it seemed an open-and-shut case. The woman had been caught in the act. The law required death by stoning—straight away. Surely Christ, by his own standards, would have to judge the woman guilty of adultery and condemn her to death as an adulterer.

But Christ steadfastly refused to assume the role of judge. Instead he assumed the role of witness. When asked for his verdict he simply said to the crowd of men around him, 'Let those of you without sin cast the first stone at her.' He witnessed to the truth, not only of her sin, but also the sin of her accusers. He then stooped and wrote something in the dust on the ground with his finger, leaving the men, baying for the woman's blood, to make their own judgment.

John 8:7–8

In encouraging these people to make their own decision, Christ took a huge risk. A woman's life was at stake. But in spite of the grave risk, Christ did not take the problem from the men and resolve it for them. He simply stayed with them and ensured they arrived at a loving solution, which was just to all the parties involved in the dispute. The men eventually made their judgment and left, one by one, from the oldest to the youngest. And the woman was left alone with Christ. 'Has no one condemned you?' he asked. 'No one, sir,' she said. Then, and only then, did Christ make his judgment. He said, 'Neither do I condemn you. Just don't do it again' (John 8:9–11). *Christ was prepared to make a judgment—but only in a way that developed people's ability to judge for themselves.*

If we are going to get involved in helping individuals or groups solve their problems, it will be extremely helpful if we understand the four steps in the problem-solving process: defining the problem; identifying all possible solutions to the problem; selecting a specific option and implementing it as the solution to the problem; and reflecting on the results of our effort to solve the problem.

- The first question that must be asked before we can even start to look for solutions is, *'What is the real problem we are facing?'* This is often the most difficult stage in problem-solving. People confuse the symptoms with the cause. Often the problem is overlaid with unresolved past conflicts. As a witness, we must help those with the problem to get beyond a superficial view to a deep understanding of what the problem is. If we cannot agree on what the problem is, then we have no chance of agreeing on a possible solution.

- The second question we need to ask is, *'What are all the possible solutions to this problem we are facing?'* At this stage it is a good idea to have a brainstorm of possible solutions. Each person thinks of as many solutions as possible and these are listed, no matter how wacky or crazy they seem. It is a good idea to ban all criticism of ideas at this stage, so that people do not feel inhibited in bringing forward their suggestions. After the list is completed, it is time to look over each solution more critically. This can be done by trying the idea out in our imagination. What would the possible results be if it were implemented? What are its weaknesses? What are its strengths? Is there some way it can be modified? There should be lots of discussion about each of the possible solutions. Disagreement will be healthy at this stage.

- The third question we need to ask is, *'Which solution will we opt for and implement?'* Those implicated in the problem must now agree on what they consider to be the best solution. The solution must be acceptable to everyone, and everyone must be convinced it has a fair chance of solving the problem. Once the solution has been chosen, the implementation has to be discussed. This involves discussing what has to be done, who will do what, and, most importantly, when it will be done. It is a good idea to break the solution down into its necessary tasks, write them all down, and beside each task write the name of the person responsible and the deadline they have agreed to. Options agreed to in principle will have no weight unless these specifics are also agreed.

- The fourth question we need to ask is, *'How is our plan to solve our problem working out?'* Reflection must take place both during and after the implementation of the solution. During the implementation, people need to get together regularly and report on how they are going with their allocated tasks. Those involved need to discuss whether the programme is actually solving the problem, or whether there needs to be some modification to the programme. Sometimes the whole programme will need to be scrapped and the whole process started again. Before starting again it will be important to discuss what was learnt from the previous effort. Why did it fail? Were we treating the symptoms or the cause? Did it fail because the solution was wrong, or because we failed to implement it properly? Experience shows that often people must be willing to 'try, try, try again' before they eventually succeed.

When the solution has been fully implemented, it is important to discuss the results. Each person should have the opportunity to say whether they feel the problem has been adequately solved. Each person should share what they have learned from the experience. Our role as witness in this problem-solving process is to help those involved work through the cycle sensibly and to be sensitive to the needs of everyone involved. *Our job is to make sure no one loses and that no one wins unless everyone wins.*

Some time back Ange and I had a phone call from a young couple whose marriage was in a no-win situation. The husband had betrayed his wife by having an affair. Even though the husband deeply regretted the hurt he had inflicted on both the other woman and his wife, the damage seemed irreparable. There were no winners, only losers. The husband had lost his integrity. The other woman had lost her dignity. The wife had lost her self-respect and her personal security. Together the husband and wife were about to lose their marriage. If the stress continued, there was a good chance one of them would lose their mind as well. So we invited them over. We sat and shared their grief and rage. Over the following weeks we spent days with them, weeping and worrying our way through the situation together. The last thing they needed was for us to take sides or give advice. Ange and I knew we couldn't take the problem from them, much as we would have loved to. They alone could solve it. All we could do was stand beside them and, in prayer, search for a way to resolve their problem, so that even if they couldn't win anything, they wouldn't lose any more than they had already lost.

It was a long struggle. There were no quick fixes, just long days and longer nights. It took time to define exactly what the problem was. There was a whole complexity of problems, some his, some hers, some theirs. It took time to sort out the tangled web. They struggled to get beyond the symptoms to the causes. They found it difficult to agree on the causes of the problems that had combined to make their married life such a misery. It took time for their hurts to heal enough for them to deal with their negative feelings about each other in a positive way. In the end, the wife took courage in her hands, forgave her husband and gave him another chance. He took the chance, and together they began to rebuild their marriage. In fact, they claim their marriage has become even stronger than it was before.

It's only in such courageous resolution of the problems—in our marriages, in our families, and in our communities—that transformation can truly take place. Ange and I once had a set of neighbours who had been feuding with each other for ten years. The problem was that one of them, whom we'll call Ben, had some banana trees growing in his backyard, which cast a shadow across his neighbour's prize vegetable patch; and the other bloke, whom we'll call Bill, used to mow his lawn at seven o'clock on a Sunday morning when his neighbour was trying to sleep off his hangover from a bout of serious heavy drinking the night before. As a result of this unresolved conflict, Ben and Bill hadn't talked to each other for the ten years leading up to the time we moved in next door to them.

Each morning I'd get up, go into my backyard, see them working in their gardens, side by side, and say, "G'day Ben! G'day Bill!" And both of them would look up, carefully, so as avoid any eye contact, say "G'day Dave!" to me, and do their best to totally ignore the bloke standing next to them at the same time. They wouldn't even give one another the time of day. We talked to them many times about resolving the conflict, but neither of them would budge. Till one day, we heard the sounds of fighting—some swearing, pushing and shoving—that ended ominously in a loud thump. Then, after a few moments' pause, someone screamed, "Bill's killed Ben!" By the time we got there it was all over. Bill was hanging over the fence, breathlessly, staring at Ben. And Ben was sprawled in a heap on the ground.

We ran to Ben to see if he was still alive. He was knocked out cold, but would live to see another day. So we carried him upstairs and laid him on his bed to recover. When he eventually came round, I said to him, 'Listen mate, you could've been killed today, all because you don't want to shift your banana trees . . . You've got to sort it out. 'Cause next time you may not be so lucky.' Ben looked at me and smiled. So I said, 'Be at my place tomorrow at three for a cup of tea and we'll sort it out.' And he nodded.

Then we jumped the fence, and went into Bill's place. He was sitting at the kitchen table with his wife who was chastising him in no uncertain terms. When she'd finished with him, I asked if I could say something. She was glad to have someone else have a go at him. And he was glad to have someone else, anyone else but her, and the fury of her anger, to contend with. So I said to him, 'Bill, you could have killed someone today, all because you want to mow the lawn at seven o'clock on a Sunday morning. You've got to sort it out. 'Cause next time you could be in big trouble, they'll toss you in jail, and throw away the key.' Bill looked at me and grimaced. So I said, 'Be at my place tomorrow at three for a cup of tea and we'll sort it out.' And he nodded.

The next day at three, bang on time, Ben and Bill turned up. I invited them in, and they sat down, looking about rather shamefacedly. As I gave them cups of tea, I caught their eye, and said, 'Well, what are we going to do?' They said nothing. Just shrugged their shoulders and sat there staring back at me. 'Well,' I said. 'It seems to me that we've got to try to end this feud before it's the end of us.' 'Yeah,' they said, looking at each other for the first time in who knew how long? 'What do you think you can do about it, Ben?' I asked. 'I could cut down my banana trees after the next bunches ripen, and replant them, further away from the fence.' 'What do you think of that, Bill?' 'That's all I want.' said Bill. 'What do you think you can do in return, Bill?' I asked. 'I guess I could mow the lawn a bit later.' 'How much later?' I asked. 'Two hours later.' 'What do you think of that, Ben?' 'That'll do me.' said Ben. 'Well I reckon we might be pretty close to a deal here. What do you reckon?' 'Sure thing!' they replied, looking pretty pleased with themselves.

'Then I've just got two final questions . . .' 'Shoot!' someone said, with an unfortunate turn of phrase. 'First question is, what are you going to do next time one or other of you comes home drunk?' Ben said, 'We don't have to hang over the fence and abuse each other. We can go to bed and sleep it off . . . as long as people let us sleep it off, that is.' 'What do you think of that, Bill?' 'Fine by me.' he said. 'So you're both happy with that?' They nodded. 'Second question is, what if something comes up? What if you get into a bit of a scrap—what are you going to do then?' Quick as a flash, Bill said, 'No worries! We'll just come over here, have a cup of tea and sort it out!' 'What do you think of that, Ben?' 'Fine by me.' he said.

From that day on, they did exactly what they said they'd do. From then on, there were no more fights. After they bore the next bunch, the banana trees were cut down. The lawn still got mown regularly on a Sunday, but later, much later, in the day. In fact, the only sound I ever heard from then on, early on a Sunday morning,

146

was the sound of Ben and Bill swapping handy hints with one another about their gardens, as they went about their work side by side. And that's what healthy community is all about.

Ideas for meditation, discussion, and action

Reflect: What problems in the community need to be resolved?

Relate: How can people bring about resolution to these problems?

Respond: Which problems are we willing to help resolve, and how?

19 Bringing About
   Prophetic Transformation

We have already noted that imparting hope is not enough to bring authentic transformation to a community. People need to be empowered to take control of their own lives. But empowerment alone is no good if people still don't understand how to use that power to resolve their problems. However, even helping people solve their own problems is not enough. They may resolve the problem in such a way that it does not contribute to the long-term development of themselves or their community. In fact, the problem may be resolved in a way that yields short-term gains but long-term losses. If authentic transformation is to occur, it is absolutely essential that people discover how to resolve their problems together in a way that yields long-term gains for everyone, even if it means short-term losses in the meantime.

In order for people to settle disputes creatively and constructively, we need to enable them to solve problems together in the light of the prophetic tradition. Throughout history there have always been prophets, both secular and religious, who have felt the heartbeat of God. These prophets courageously speak to us, in sympathy with God, about God's passion for love and justice. They call on society to grow and change by solving problems in the light of God's agenda: to develop a world in which all resources will be shared equally among all people, so that even the most disadvantaged among us will be able to meet their basic needs with dignity and joy. But history is the story of the silencing of the prophet, and hence the silencing of God himself. In rejecting the voice of God, history has become a tale of paradise lost, revolutions betrayed and lives wasted. If genuine, sustainable transformation is to occur, we must enable people to solve their problems together in a way which takes into account the essential, visionary insights of the prophetic tradition. It is impossible to create a more loving and just society unless we take into account the agenda of love and justice advocated by sages throughout the ages.

Living at the time of Christ were two men who had a problem they wanted to resolve. Both were rich, while most of those around them lived in dire poverty, struggling for survival. One was an aristocrat, the other an extortionist. Both felt uncomfortable about the disparity between their luxurious life style and the destitution they saw around them. Both decided they didn't like this discomfort, and decided to do something about it. Both decided they would get a third party to help them solve their problem. Both sought out Christ, a recognised prophet.

The rich young aristocrat ignored the advice advocated by Christ. It may have been a good ideal to give everything to the poor, but it wasn't a good idea for *him*. Not that he didn't want to give to the poor. He just needed to keep a solid capital base to do it. He did not want to waste his capital on unprofitable charities. He probably rationalised his decision by arguing it was the most sensible course of action. He decided to solve his problem, not by giving away his wealth, but by simply refusing to feel guilty about it. If he had any guilt feelings left, I'm sure his priest and psychotherapist helped him cope. The old extortionist, on the other hand, decided to handle his problem a different way. He followed the advice of Christ. He gave half his wealth to the poor and repaid all those he had ripped off, not just what he had taken, but four times as much, as a form of compensation.

Matthew 19:16-22, Luke 19:1-10

Both these men had effectively resolved their problem, one by accepting the imperatives of the prophetic tradition, the other by rejecting them. By ignoring the advice of Christ to share his wealth with the poor, the aristocrat chose a solution that upheld his right to dispose of his private property as he chose, *over against* the rights of the poor to access the resources he had at his disposal to meet their basic human needs. In so doing, the aristocrat chose to solve his problem at the expense of the poor. There were short-term gains for the aristocrat, but long-term losses for the rest of the community. On the other hand, by taking the advice of Christ to share his wealth with the poor, the extortionist chose a solution that upheld his right to dispose of his private property as he so chose, *as well as* the rights of the poor to access the resources he had at his disposal. In so doing, the extortionist chose to solve the problem at his own expense. There were short-term losses, like having to give away half of his wealth to the poor, and pay back every dollar he swindled to people, at the rate of four to one. But the short-term losses would result in long-term gains for everybody in the community, including the extortionist. The poor would get some unexpected social security payments; the extortionist's victims would get the compensation they'd always hoped for, but never expected to get; and the extortionist would get back some self-respect, now he was no longer an extortionist.

I am convinced that genuine, sustainable transformation can only be brought about by enabling people to solve their problems together in the light of the prophetic tradition, perfectly personified in the life of Jesus the Christ. That being so, we need to find a way to facilitate this process of transformation by enabling people to solve their problems together in the light of the life of Christ. With those who acknowledge Christ to some degree or other, it is reasonably straightforward. When we meet together we encourage each other to share our problems and to help each other resolve these problems in the light of the prophetic tradition. We acknowledge the problems we are trying to solve. We discuss the issues with the people who share the problems we are trying to solve. Then we search the Scriptures in general, and the life of Christ in particular, to discover a story that reveals how God may want us to resolve the problem in the light of his passion for love and justice. This process results in an intimate acquaintance with the heart of God, which enables us to resolve our problems in a way that reflects the heart of God.

This is all very well, but the real challenge is to facilitate the same kind of process with the majority of people who, for a whole range of reasons, do not acknowledge Christ as a significant figure in their lives. Let me tell you how I try to do it. Most of the people I work with in the community do not claim to be Christians. In fact some are decidedly anti-Christian. But I agree to work with them on the understanding that our decisions be on the basis of common sense and consensus. Because God is the source of truth, and that truth is written on the hearts of all people (Romans 2:14–15) and living in the hearts of all people (John 1:9), that truth is often expressed in the common sense we speak to each other. Quite often, to the embarrassment of those Christians who claim exclusive rights to truth, those who do not claim to be Christian have a clearer understanding of the truth.

Whenever somebody says something which I believe is true to the heart of God, I agree with it. If I do not believe it is in tune with

God's heart, I disagree with it. Just because I disagree doesn't automatically mean I will voice my disagreement. Conflict, like kisses, should be saved for special occasions. The way I see it, every time I agree, I gain a credit in credibility. Every time, I disagree I lose a credit. I want to gain credibility to discuss crucial issues, not lose credibility over incidental issues. I save my credits for the time I need to spend them on a disagreement that is substantive. However, I don't find myself in disagreement as much as others might imagine. I find I can usually, if not invariably, agree with the way sensible people decide to solve their problems. The times I do find myself in disagreement, I feel perfectly free to express my thoughts because we have agreed to resolve our problems by consensus, which means no-one coerces anyone else into agreeing on any course of action with which they disagree.

In practice I find that many groups I work with, even those who only use God's name blasphemously, often act in sympathy with his heart. That may seem strange to some. But it may not seem so strange if we remember that all of us, even those of us who don't believe in God, are made in the image of God, an image which though distorted, has not been totally destroyed by our proclivity to stupidity. So together we can agree to solve problems according to God's agenda—though at the time I may be the only one to recognise it as such.

Once we have resolved a problem and we are rejoicing together, I make explicit the implicit connection between the decision we have made and the prophetic tradition personified in Christ. I love to tell people, particularly those hostile to Christianity, who are celebrating the successful resolution of a problem, that the success was dependent on our having taken the kind of action Jesus Christ advocated. Regardless of their attitudes to Christ, they cannot deny the successful resolution of the problem or disregard the value of the kind of action advocated by Christ—especially when they have just tried it and seen how well it works!

I go through this process over and over again. Each time the group makes significant progress towards personal growth and social change, and each time I explain the significance of God's agenda personified in Christ to the process we have just experienced. As a result, God's agenda increasingly becomes a more credible *point of view*. Sooner or later—usually later—God's agenda, personified in Christ, becomes such a credible point of view that it moves from being one among many that are credible, to the one by which all others are judged. The indicator that this time has arrived is when people ask about God's agenda *before* they make a decision rather than *after*. At this stage it is crucial to know enough about the prophetic tradition in general, and the gospels in particular, to be able to find a parable, a story or a principle that relates directly to the problem the group is seeking to resolve.

If people adopt the agenda of God, personified in Christ, as the agenda for their decision-making, they have made a significant transition. The agenda of God has moved from being a point of view to the point of reference. The process of conversion to Christ as a person—not necessarily Christianity as a religion—has begun. And part and parcel of this conversion process, is the incredible potential for authentic, sustainable, community transformation.

Let me tell you a story of how such a process took place among a group of people who were not only non-Christians, but decidedly anti-Christian. Together with my friends, we decided to get involved with a bunch of squatters. They were totally demoralised. They had no jobs. With no jobs they could not afford to pay rent. Because they had nowhere to live, they squatted on land beside the road. Because this was illegal, they were constantly harassed by the police, who would either demand a bribe, or break down their hutments and beat them up. As a result they were constantly on the move, trying desperately to stay one step ahead of the police. But there weren't many places they could go, so they always wound up back where they started, ready to go through the cycle again.

We got to know this group. Bonds of friendship formed between individuals and their families. What they lacked in dignity, they more than made up for in guts. Their struggle against seemingly overwhelming odds was fought with lots of courage and lots of laughter. We were encouraged and strengthened by their infectious style of heroism and sense of humour. They may have been demoralised, but they taught us valuable lessons about morality. As our friendships deepened, we not only learned from them the art of survival in an urban slum, we began to feel the anguish they felt in their struggle to survive. As we discussed with them the issues they had to face every day of their lives, we decided to work together with them and see if together we could find some long-term solutions that would not only minimise the anguish associated with their struggle for survival, but also increase their chances of surviving.

One day the group decided something had to be done about the continuing police harassment. Some wanted to attack the police station immediately with bricks. Bricks were a common means of settling disputes in the slum. As a conflict resolution technique, the people considered it a knockout. We encouraged the people to envisage in their minds what the result of throwing bricks through the window of the police station might be. They concluded that it would probably result in an even more violent visit by the police. The people began to have very serious doubts about the effectiveness of bricks as a conflict resolution technique.

So we began to discuss other possibilities for solving the problem. Someone suggested inviting the police over for a cup of tea and discussing the matter. The squatters treated the idea with scorn, but we supported it. The longer we discussed it, the more support it got. Eventually the police were invited. To start with, you could cut the air with a knife, but the tension was soon dispelled with a couple of jokes. The squatters and the police ended up having an amicable chat and as a result decided to call a truce. The squatters agreed not to cause the police any trouble and the police agreed not to beat up the squatters.

After the police had gone, we had a talk about how the problem had been resolved. During the discussion one of us mentioned that the problem had been resolved exactly as Christ had suggested. He said, 'Bless those who curse you' and 'If your enemy is thirsty, give him a drink', which is exactly what the group had done by inviting the police for a cup of tea. Everyone treated it as a joke. They were embarrassed that they had done anything remotely religious, even if unintentionally. But the squatters remembered the way they had solved the problem with the police and they also remembered that it was the way Christ suggested problems be solved.

Time went by. Week after week, month after month, we worked on a whole range of problems together: everything from getting a regular water supply to improving nutrition and sanitation. Each time we resolved a problem together it would be on the basis of common sense and consensus. After the effective resolution of each of these problems, we would discuss how the decision we had taken, fitted with the way Christ advocated for dealing with problems. After each successful resolution of a problem there would be a celebration. It was during this euphoria that we would always explain how the success was contingent upon our having worked in harmony with God's agenda, as personified in Christ; and always there would be the mock groans, that if we carried on the way we were going, that they would all be Christians before too long!

About a year after inviting the police for a cup of tea, the council decided to clean up the city. Cleaning up the city meant getting rid of the squatters. They were notified to leave immediately. But they had nowhere to go. Then they got news that really freaked them out. The bulldozers were on the way. In a panic they considered their options. But there didn't seem to be any. Any promising options had to be discarded because they felt too powerless to make them happen. 'It's typical,' they concluded. 'Those big people can push us little people around as much as they like and there is not a thing we can do about it.' We were tempted to agree. Things looked hopeless. But somehow we knew that we had to believe that the impossible was possible.

'Surely there is *something* we can do!' one person said hopefully. 'Yeah?' asked one of the squatters. 'What? What would Christ do about it?' Raising Christ, as a possible point of reference for solving the problem, had never happened before in our discussions with the squatters. It was a crucial time for this group: a time when Christ might become more than just one among many points of view; a time when Christ might become the point of reference for all their problem solving, when the group might be converted to a faith in Christ through which their life might be transformed. It all hinged upon finding a Christ story that the group could use to help them to *do* something about their situation. I racked my brain, wondering where on earth you could find a story in the gospels that helped a group of squatters deal with the threat of eviction backed by the might of bulldozers.

I don't remember who it was, but someone suggested a story they thought might help. It was the story Christ told of a little old widow who was finding it difficult to get justice from a big crooked judge. She finally got justice by knocking on his door at all hours of the night for week after week. As we discussed the story with them, hope began to rise out of their hopelessness. As hope was born, so was a new sense of power. They started discussing the possible solutions in a whole new light. They decided to take up a petition to present to the city council and to persist until they got a fair hearing. They gathered hundreds of signatures and organised a march to the city council administration centre to present the petitions. Then they followed up on the people who could change the decision. Finally, through perseverance they had learned about in the story of the little old widow and the big crooked judge, they were granted an alternative place to stay where the community would have their own houses on their own land. Not only that, the council would help pay the expenses of their move. It was more than they had ever dreamed possible.

The move also opened up a whole host of new doors. Not only did they now have their own homes on their own land, they could now develop their own education, health and employment programmes. With the decrease in demoralisation came an observable increase in morale, and morality, in the community. There was a marked decrease in domestic violence and child abuse. People engaged in more constructive forms of work, and less destructive forms of recreation. There was a marked increase in happier couples and healthier children. Fewer people went to untimely graves. And those who survived not only lived longer, they also lived fuller lives. And at the centre of all this activity was a group in the community who remembered that the personal growth and social change had come about because they had followed the agenda of God, personified in Christ. This group weren't content with their growth so far. They looked into the future, and saw some of the changes that were possible, if they were to follow in the footsteps of Christ, and, like him, live wholeheartedly for God, and his agenda of love and justice.

Ideas for meditation, discussion, and action

Reflect: What constitutes authentic, sustainable transformation?

Relate: How crucial is conversion to this process of transformation?

Respond: What do we need to do to bring about prophetic transformation?

From Half-Hearted to Wholehearted Humanity

Not for me portfolios -
  Stocks of silver, pots of gold.
Not for me a treasure trove -
  Sparklin' jewels so bright but cold.

Not for me a fancy home -
  Sumptuous mansion, spacious lawn.
Not for me a garden gnome -
  Sitting pretty, all alone.

Not for me a life of style -
  Gin and tonic, suit and tie.
Not for me a plastic smile -
  Making love an empty lie.

Give me purpose. Give me passion.
  Give me patience too.
Human feeling. Human being.
  Human doing good.

'Not For Me' from the album Wonder Come *by Dave Andrews*

A Sayings that can Stir the Heart

The sayings of Christ confront us with truth straight from the heart of God. Nothing challenges our opinions and prejudices or calls us to a cause of pure compassion more than these sayings. The following section is not a theoretical look at these sayings, but a practical introduction to the way these sayings can help us change ourselves and change our world.

The sayings of Christ are simple and practical; simple enough to understand, practical enough for anyone to put them into practice. To *quote* the sayings of Christ is religious—but to *act* on them is revolutionary. Whenever the sayings are not translated into action they are reduced to meaningless clichés; a religious rhetoric about unrealised ideals that are worse than useless in a world which is sick and tired of a piety that refuses to roll its sleeves up and lend a hand to those in need. However, when the sayings of Christ are translated into action, the ideals become ideas that work; a divine agenda for radical yet viable, personal growth and social change which enables us to work towards the realisation of our dreams for a better world.

For example, Greg Manning, a friend who works with people infected with HIV, has taken the sayings of Christ as guidelines for developing a healing approach to 'positive' people. Greg says that developing a 'healing' approach is vital because 'the absence of a cure for AIDS is not the only reason why people with HIV die.' Greg says, 'People who are "positive" can be "healed" of sickness again and again, and the "healing" is a crucial part of preventing transmission'.

Greg has taken eight sayings of Christ in particular, as guidelines for his work.

- When his disciples, faced with a disabled man, asked the question 'Who was it that sinned to cause this disability?' Christ replied: *'Neither this man nor his parents sinned, but that the works of God should be revealed in him'* (John 9:3). Considering this saying, Greg says, 'Blaming people for their problems is an effective way of excusing ourselves from compassionate involvement. Blaming people for HIV infection is still a common perspective. Jesus' disciples used the reason of sin to explain to themselves a man's suffering. They wanted to know whose fault it was. [However] Jesus urged his disciples to reconsider the way they saw the man, and to look for the works of God revealed in that man. As we encounter people who are affected by HIV, we will do well to consider how the works of God might be revealed in these people, rather than trying to find some one to blame for their condition'.
- When a man with a disability asked Christ for help and Christ's helpers told to him to shut up, Christ scolded his disciples for their disrespect and then said unequivocally, *'Call him'* (Mark10:49). Considering this saying, Greg says, 'Some people are discouraged from accessing treatment and receiving healing. Drug users are one group of people who are often discouraged from accessing health care if they have not overcome their chemical addiction. As Jesus went past Bartimaeus, the people warned the blind man to be quiet, but Jesus heard him, and called him over. We [too] must facilitate access to health care to people who are excluded'.
- When the man with a disability came over, Christ said, *'What do you want me to do for you?'* (Mark 10:51) Considering this saying,

Greg says, 'The design of some health care services may be inappropriate for the needs of particular sections of the population. Jesus asked this supposedly troublesome man a very open question, "What do you want me to do for you?" Bartimaeus' request to receive his sight may have seemed impossible to some. Jesus sent him away seeing, and saying, "Your faith has made you well." When we ask people who are most at risk of HIV infection Jesus' question, their response also may seem [to demand] the impossible. But people who have difficulty gaining access to health care need to be involved in the design of new structures and protocols, which they can access and effectively use for their own healing.'

- When Christ had gone out of his way to talk to a sick man who had not been able to access any health services, no matter how hard he had tried, Christ walked up and asked him, *'Do you want to be made well?'* (John 5:6) Considering this saying, Greg says, 'It is not possible for some people to get access to treatment and healing on their own. The healing of people who have been abandoned or imprisoned can depend upon the initiative of someone else. Jesus saw one such man lying beside a pool, hoping for healing. Jesus learnt of the man's condition and that he had been there for a long time. He approached him and asked him, *"Do you want to be made well?"* The man's response to Jesus led to his healing. Jesus' initiative with the man beside the pool is a model for his followers.'

- When Christ tried to help someone, but wanted to check whether the outcome was okay or not, in the middle of the intervention he asked the blind man he was helping, *'What do you see?'* (Mark 8:23) Considering this saying, Greg says, 'Sometimes, people tell health care workers what they think the worker wants to hear. This may take the form of saying that they have been healed of something that, in fact, is still troubling them. A person who has not complied with advice, may be particularly fearful of being reprimanded or denied future access to the service. Jesus asked a blind man what he saw after Jesus first touched him. The man was not seeing what Jesus wanted him to see, so he touched him again. Healing is recognised by the outcome. We must encourage and enable people to describe themselves accurately and fearlessly. They must know that we are committed to good outcomes and able to overcome complications'.

- After healing a man with a disability, Christ looked at the man and said, *'Your faith has made you whole'* (Mark 10:52). Considering this saying, Greg says, 'Sometimes, it can be very difficult for a person to seek healing. For example, successfully treating tuberculosis can require considerable resolve and encouragement over a long period of time. A person who has a sexually transmitted infection may feel ashamed to disclose their condition and seek healing. Jesus often affirmed people's faith when he responded to their health-seeking behaviour. He would say to the people whom he healed, "Your faith has made you well." The explicit affirmation of someone who is trying to care for their health is an important aspect of healing for a person, for both the present and the future.'

- After healing a woman who had been sick for twelve years, Christ said to her, *'Go in peace'* (Mark 5:34). Considering this saying, Greg says, 'HIV infection will often involve recurrent illness. It can be particularly discouraging to have painful, embarrassing or debilitating things that we don't expect or understand repeatedly happen to our bodies. Much of what happens to our bodies can be healed. After healing one woman who had a chronic condition, which had caused her to spend all that she had on twelve years of visits to numerous physicians, Jesus sent her off with the words, "Go in peace." People need to be encouraged. When an incident of healing ends with a gesture of peace, a person is more likely to stay healthy for longer and to return for healing when it is next required.'

- When he was talking to his disciples about what it meant to be blessed, and to be a blessing to others, Christ said to them, *'Blessed are those who mourn for they shall be comforted'* (Matthew 5:4). Considering this saying, Greg says, 'HIV infection can lead to a great sense of loss. These losses might include the loss of health, the loss of strength or resolve, the loss of employment, the loss of family and friends, the loss of home, the loss of dreams of the future and perhaps even the loss of faith. Those who actively work for the healing of these people, are the "blessing of God", who comforts the distressed'.

Like Greg, we can take the sayings of Christ and translate these sayings into guidelines for action in our lives, by following these steps:

1. Select a saying that speaks to our situation. 'Which of Christ's sayings is relevant to my situation?'
2. Meditate on that saying. 'What does Christ's saying tell me about how he would approach my situation?' Ask the question and listen carefully, imaginatively and creatively for the answer.
3. Translate the saying into action. 'How could I approach my situation in the way Christ would?' Experiment with the truth. Practise the love and justice which are the heart of the saying.
4. Reflect on the translation. 'Did I really take the heart of the saying to heart?' Evaluate the experiment with truth and try again. Remember that practice makes perfect.

Sayings about truth, love and justice

There is only one who is good: God. *Matthew 19:17*

You must be as good as God. *Matthew 5:38*

Beware of the experts. *Luke 20:46*

Why don't you judge what's right? *Luke 12:57*

Stop judging by people appearances, and make good righteous judgements. *John 7:24*

What the world regards highly is disgusting to God. *Luke 16:15*

Everyone who exalts himself, will be humbled. Everyone who humbles himself, will be exalted. *Luke 18:14*

Those who are last, will be first. Those who are first, will be last. *Luke 13:30*

How sad it is for you, who neglect to do justice. *Luke 11:42*

How sad it is for you, who load people down with burdens they cannot bear, and you will not even lift a finger to help. *Luke 11:46*

How sad it is, because of the things that cause people to sin. *Matthew 18:7*

The temptation to do wrong is inevitable, but how sad it is for those of you through whom temptation comes to others. *Matthew 18:7*

How happy are the pure in heart, for they will see God. *Matthew 5:8*

How happy are those who seek justice, for they will be satisfied. *Matthew 5:6*

How happy are those who are persecuted for righteousness, for God's new world order of justice will be just right for them. *Matthew 5:10*

How happy are those who manage their affairs fairly, for they will have the whole earth as their heritage. *Matthew 5:5*

Sayings about simplicity, solidarity and service

Love the Lord your God with all your heart, with all your soul, with all your body, and with all your mind.   *Luke 10:27*

Give to the government what belongs to the government; give to God what belongs to God—whatever bears the mark of God.
                                                                      Matthew 22:21

You can either serve God or Money. But you cannot serve both.
                                                                      Matthew 6:24

Be on guard against all kinds of greed.   *Luke 12:15*

Be careful, lest you let your hearts will be overwhelmed by self-indulgence, drunkenness, and distractions in life.   *Luke 12:15*

Don't be troubled about tomorrow; tomorrow can take care of itself. The troubles of today will always be enough for today.
                                                                      Matthew 6:34

Who of you by worrying, can add a single hour to your life? Since you cannot even do this, why worry about the rest?
                                                                      Luke 12:25–26

Do not be anxious about your life, about what you can get to eat or drink. Is not life, itself, immeasurably more important than its nourishment?   *Matthew 6:25*

What good is it, if someone gains the whole world, and loses their soul?   *Matthew 16:26*

Give to anyone who asks for anything. If anyone wants to borrow something, let them have it.   *Matthew 5:42*

If anyone takes anything of yours, don't ask for it back. *Luke 6:30*

Share—without expecting something back in return. *Luke 6:35*

Sell everything you have, and give it to those don't have anything.   *Luke 18:22*

How sad it is for the rich, for you have received your comfort.
                                                                      Luke 6:24

How happy are the poor in spirit, for God's movement is for them. *Matthew 5:3*

How sad it is for you that are well fed now, for you will go hungry. *Luke 6:25*

How happy are you that hunger now, for you will be well fed. *Luke 6:21*

How sad it is for you who laugh now, for you will weep. *Luke 6:25*

How happy are those who weep now, for you will laugh. *Luke 6:21*

Sayings about compassion, acceptance and respect

God is compassionate—even to people who don't appreciate it. Be as compassionate as God is—even if people don't appreciate it. *Luke 6:35–36*

Don't make a show of your religion in order to attract attention. *Matthew 6:1*

Whenever you do someone a favour, don't tell the world about it. *Matthew 6:3*

Always treat other people just as you would like them to treat you. *Matthew 7:12*

How happy are those who cry, for they will be comforted. *Matthew 5:4*

How happy are those who show mercy, for they will be shown mercy. *Matthew 5:7*

Whoever would like to be a leader should be willing to be a servant. *Matthew 20:26*

When you are invited to a special function, do not take the best seat. *Luke 14:8*

When you put on a party, don't invite your rich neighbours and relations. But make sure you invite the poor, the disabled, and the disadvantaged. *Luke 14:12–13*

Treat older people with respect. *Luke 18:20*

Do not treat kids with contempt. *Matthew 18:10*

Love your neighbour as yourself. *Luke 10:27*

Sayings about conflict, confrontation and suffering

In the world, the way it is, you are going to have big trouble. *John 16:33*

How sad are you, when all people speak well of you, for that is how people always speak about false prophets. *Luke 6:26*

How happy are you, when people despise you, and insult you, and exclude you, because you want to follow the way of Christ. *Luke 6:22*

You will cry while the world rejoices. But your grief will turn to joy. *John 16:20*

You will rejoice—and no one will be able to take away your joy. *John 16:22*

Do not put your trust in untrustworthy people. *Matthew 10:17*

A good tree yields good fruit, and a bad tree yields bad fruit. By their fruit, you will know whether people are good, or bad. *Matthew 7:17,20*

How happy are the peacemakers, for they are the children of God. *Matthew 5:9*

Be as shrewd as it is possible to be—but always be peaceful. *Matthew 10:16*

Don't react violently against those who will try to attack you. If anyone hits you on one cheek, turn the other cheek. *Matthew 5:39*

Do good to all people, even to those who do evil to you. Love those who hate you. Bless those who curse you. *Matthew 5:44*

In resolving a conflict, begin by getting the plank out of your own eye, before you start trying to take the speck out of someone else's eye. *Matthew 7:3*

If someone does something wrong, take them to task. If they are sorry, forgive them. If someone does something wrong seven times a day, and if they come back seven times a day, and say they are sorry, forgive them. *Luke 17:3–4*

If someone wrongs you, go and show them their fault between you and them alone. If they listen to you, you have saved your friendship. But if they will not listen to you, take one or two others with you, that every word may be confirmed on the evidence of two or three witnesses. If they refuse to listen to them, tell it to the community. If they pay no attention to the community, you just have to treat them like a stranger. *Matthew 18:17*

Let the dead bury the dead. *Matthew 8:22*

Don't be afraid of those who can kill the body but not the soul. *Matthew 10:28*

A woman giving birth to a child has pain. But when the baby is born she forgets the anguish because of the joy that a child has been born. *John 16:21*

Sayings about power, possibility and responsibility

With God anything is possible. *Matthew 19:26*

Don't make a move until you have been infused with power from God. *Luke 24:49*

Nothing shall be impossible to you.   *Matthew 17:20*

Happy are those who believe without seeing.   *John 20:29*

Happy are those who hear the word of God and obey it.

Luke 11:28

Unless a person is willing to start their life all over again, they cannot be a part of God's emerging new world order.   *John 3:3*

Follow me.   *Matthew 8:22*

If anyone wishes to follow in my footsteps, you must disregard your life, and be ready to die.   *Matthew 16:24*

Whoever is concerned about saving their life, will lose it; but whoever loses their life, for my sake, will save it. *Matthew 10:39*

God's emerging new world order is here—and now—in you.

Luke 17:21

Don't tell anyone, but show them, and let them see for themselves.   *Luke 5:14*

As long as it's day we must work. Night is coming when no one can work.   *John 9:4*

Set your heart on God's agenda and the justice at the heart of it.

Matthew 6:33

Those of you who are willing to do justice will shine like the sun.   *Matthew 13:43*

You—yes, you—are the light of the world.   *Matthew 5:14*

Let your light so shine, that people may see the good that you do and honour the One who brings the good things of heaven to earth.   *Matthew 5:16*

B Stories that can Inspire the Heart

The stories Christ told, and the stories told about Christ, can be an invaluable resource for those who want to be involved in working for growth and change. Like a road map for a traveller exploring unfamiliar territory, they give us direction. I once suggested to my father, a preacher of note who teaches potential preachers how to preach, that the best thing he could do for the community was proclaim a moratorium on preaching. He was horrified but kindly asked me to explain. I told him I thought the time could be used better by getting the large congregation to break up into small groups to study the stories of Christ and seek to live out the storylines in their own lives. I am convinced that it is only as we allow the stories of Christ to reframe our involvement in the community that we will be able to practise what we preach.

My father never did proclaim a moratorium on preaching, but both of us have done our best to help groups of people study the stories of Christ. Both of us have tried to help people relate to these stories as road maps to be followed, rather than picture postcards to be admired. And as people have followed the directions laid out in these stories, they have found themselves inevitably following the footsteps of Christ into the struggle for love and justice in our community.

I have developed some studies of the stories of Christ that have been helpful to groups I have worked with. While they are designed primarily for small groups, individuals can also use them. Here are some simple guidelines to get the most out of these studies:

1 Begin with prayer.
2 Read the questions.
3 Trust the Spirit.
4 Listen to the answers.
5 Take your time.
6 Discourage any one person in the group from dominating.
7 Encourage people not to debate with each other but to understand one another.
8 Avoid side-tracks by suggesting that side issues be discussed over coffee later.
9 If there is difficulty, acknowledge it, but still try to answer the questions.
10 End with the exercise suggested.

The Spirit of Christ

(Requirements - paper and pen)

Discussion

1 What purpose do we believe God has for us? Write it down.
2 Read about the purpose Jesus believed the Spirit of God had for him.

Jesus came to Nazareth, the little town where he had been brought up, and went to the synagogue on the sabbath like he always did. An attendant asked him to share something from the Old Book. So he read the manifesto, written by a prophet called Isaiah, for the long-awaited leader. 'The Spirit of God has got hold of me, and is urging me to take on a special task; to share good news with the poor; free the prisoners; help the handicapped; and smash the shackles of the oppressed.' Then

Jesus closed the book, handed it back to the attendant, and sat down. Well, you could have heard a pin drop. All the people stared at him. So he looked around at them all and said, 'Today this vision has become a reality. I have made this manifesto my own!'

Luke 4:20–21

3   Compare this sense of purpose with ours. What are the similarities? What are the differences? Why?
4   How do we think Jesus understood the Nazareth Manifesto? What kind of involvement with people did it mean for Jesus?
5   Who are the 'poor' in our world today?
6   What would be good news for these people?
7   Who are the 'prisoners' in our world?
8   How can we work for their release?
9   Who are the 'handicapped' in our world?
10   How can we help them live their lives more fully?
11   Who are the 'oppressed' in our society?
12   How can we break the shackles of the oppressed?
13   What is the source of the power for the struggle for justice?
14   How is the power of the Spirit different from other kinds of power?
15   How can we derive strength from the power of the Spirit?

Action

Let's read what we wrote at the beginning of the study about our sense of purpose again. Then let's read what Jesus said in the Nazareth Manifesto about his sense of purpose again. Let's reconsider our understanding of our mission in the light of Christ's understanding of his mission. Let's open our hearts to the inspiration of the Spirit of God, and prayerfully re-write a manifesto for our own lives, in the light of the Nazareth Manifesto. Then let's share our manifesto with others. After sharing our manifestos with one another, let's spend a few minutes, over a cup of coffee, talking about the implications of these manifestos for the way we will live our lives, individually and collectively, from now on.

The principle of justice
(Requirements - paper and pen)

Discussion
1 Define justice, and draw a picture that illustrates our idea of justice.
2 Show the picture to the group and discuss your ideas of justice.
3 Read the parable of the sheep and the goats told by Jesus:

When the Human One comes, all the nations will be gathered before him, and he will separate the people one from another as a shepherd separates the sheep from the goats. He will put the sheep—who have done right—on his right, and the goats— who haven't—on his left. Then the True Leader will say to those on his right, 'Come, join the party. For I was hungry and you gave me a feed. I was thirsty and you gave me a drink. I had just arrived in town and you took me into your home. My clothes were in tatters and you gave me your own outfit. I was sick in bed and you came and spent time with me. I was stuck in prison and you were there for me and my family.' Stunned, the people on the right will say to him, 'When on earth did we see you hungry and give you a feed, or thirsty and give you a drink? When did we meet you after you had just arrived in town and give you a bed for the night? When were you sick in bed and we spent time with you? When were you stuck in prison and we were there for you and your family?' The True Leader will say, 'Whenever you did the right thing by those whom most consider least, you did the right thing by me!'

Then, turning to those on his left, the True Leader will say, 'Get out. You can go to hell with everyone else who has made life hell for others. I was hungry and you never gave me a feed; thirsty and you never gave me a drink; lonely, without a friend, and you walked by; half-naked and you didn't give me any clothes; sick in bed, and stuck in jail, and you didn't even visit.' And those who are left will be bewildered, and say, 'When did we see you hungry or thirsty? When did we see you without a friend or without clothes? When did we see you sick in bed or stuck in prison?' And the True Leader will say to them, 'Whenever you did not do the right thing by those whom most consider least, you did not do the right thing by me!'

Matthew 25:31-46

4   Both the 'sheep' and the 'goats' were surprised at the connection Jesus made between the way they had treated those whom most consider least and the True Leader. Why do you think that was so?

5   What are our reactions to Jesus' suggestion that, on Judgment Day, we will all be judged by the way we have treated the poor?

6   What is the principle by which we will all be judged?

7   Who are those that most consider least in our society?

8   How can we treat them so that we do them justice?

9   In what ways are we most likely *not* to do the right thing by those in the community that most consider least?

10 What excuses do we usually use to rationalise our failures?

11 What do we imagine God's response will be to our rationalisations?

12 How can we make sure we succeed more often than we fail in doing the right thing by those in the community that most consider least?

Action

Let's spend some time thinking about a specific choice we are faced with at the moment. Who do we normally discount in making such a choice? How could we make this choice so as to do justice to those we usually don't take into account? Let's share some of our dilemmas with the group and discuss together how we might be able to resolve them.

The light in the darkness

(Requirements - paper and pen, a candle, and a room that can be darkened)

Discussion

1 Turn off the lights or darken the room and discuss the question: How does being in darkness make us feel?

2 Light a candle. How does it affect us when we are trapped in the darkness and someone lights a candle?

3 Read the following statement by Jesus:

You are the world's light. It is impossible to hide a town built on the top of a hill.

Have you ever heard of anyone lighting a candle and putting it under the table? Don't you put it on a candlestick on the table so it gives light to the whole room? Well then, since you

are the world's light, go ahead and shine so brightly that when people see the good things you do they'll thank God.
Matthew 5:14–16

4   What is the 'darkness', in us, and around us?

5   Who does Jesus say are 'the light of the world'?

6   Why does Jesus insist we can be 'the light of the world'?

7   How does the idea of being the light of the world make us feel?

8   When we think of what we have to offer the world, what do we think would describe it best—a candle, a sixty-watt light bulb or a flood light? Why?

9   What would make us want to hide our 'light' under the table?

10 In his statement, Jesus says that our light is in the good things we do. Why did Jesus say that the light the world is reflected best, not in our good words, but in our good deeds?

11 Think of the good things others have done in our community. Which of these do we think effectively confronted the darkness and infused light into our community?

12 Think of one good thing we could do in our neighbourhood that would bring some light into the darkness.

Action

Let's share with the group about the one good thing we would like to do. Think of the excuses we have used to 'hide our light' in the past, and talk about how we can overcome the temptation to do it again in the future. Then let's form a circle around the candle, and pray to God to help us make our light shine, rather than curse the darkness in our world.

The yeast in the flour

(Requirements - paper and pen; flour, yeast, and water, and a bowl)

Discussion

1   Have someone knead the flour, yeast, and water into dough.
2   Then put the dough in the bowl on one side to let it rise.
3   Read the following short statement:

Jesus told them another illustration: 'The movement of God is like yeast ,which a woman took and mixed into a large amount of flour until the whole had risen.'
   Matthew 13:33

4   Why did Jesus use this image to illustrate the way God's movement operates?
5   If we used this image as a model for the role of believers in their neighbourhood, who would we identify as the yeast and who would we identify as the flour? Why?
6   What does the 'yeast' have to offer to the 'flour'?
7   What can we offer to our neighbourhood?
8   What does the 'flour' have to offer the 'yeast'?
9   What can our neighbourhood offer to us?
10 How must the yeast and the flour be combined if the bread is to rise properly?
11 How can we, as believers, be as well integrated into our neighbourhood as that?
12 Why does Jesus insist that the significance of the yeast is seen, not in the difference between the yeast and the flour, but in the difference the yeast makes with the flour to the combined mixture?
13 What difference do we make to our community?

14 According to this illustration, what is the most effective way in which believers could make a difference in our neighbourhoods?

Action

Let's think of one way we can become 'yeast' in our neighbourhoods. Let's decide how we can do it, then break into pairs, share our decision with our partner and make arrangements to contact each other within seven days to see how we are going with it.

The people's organisation

(Requirements - paper and pen, a whiteboard and a whiteboard marker)

Discussion

1 Draw a line down the middle of the whiteboard, and on the right-hand side have someone draw a normal organisational pyramid chart.

2 What do we notice about the organisational pyramid? Where are the bosses located? Where are the workers located? What is the relationship between the bosses and the workers? Why are the bosses on top and the workers on the bottom?

3 Read what Jesus has to say about 'bosses' and 'workers':

We all know bosses call the shots and heavies like to throw their weight around. But that's *not* the way you should do things. If you want to be a leader, don't act like a boss, let others call the shots; don't throw your weight around like a heavy, but do the hard work yourself. For the True Leader didn't come to be waited on hand and foot, but to be a worker, spending his life serving others, so that others could have a life worth living.

Matthew 20:25–28

4 What does Jesus say about organisations where bosses are on the top and workers are on the bottom?

5 What does Jesus suggest is a better form of organisation?

6 On the left hand side of the whiteboard have some people draw a chart of the organisation Jesus had in mind. Is it an inverted pyramid? A simple flat structure? A series of intersecting circles? Or something else?

7 What are the similarities and differences between the traditional and the alternative organisation?

8 What are the strengths and weaknesses of the traditional style?

9 What are the strengths and weaknesses of the alternative style?

10 What style of organisation would we prefer to work with? Why?

11 Why did Jesus insist on our being workers rather than bosses?

Action

Let's get in a circle and spend some time answering two crucial questions. One: how can we act more like workers, and less like bosses, in our office, our church, our locality and our family? Two: what processes and structures can we set up to empower the disempowered paid and unpaid workers in our community groups? Then, let's talk over the answers we have to these questions, and make some plans to help each other develop some real people's organisations in our community.

The radical agenda

(Requirements - paper and pen, a table and some money in our pockets)

Discussion

1   Read the following story that shows the 'radical agenda' Jesus set for people:

A man came up to Jesus and put it to him, 'Teacher, what do I need to do to be okay from here on out?' Jesus said, 'Why ask me? If you want to live life as you ought to, just obey the rules for living.' 'What rules?' the man enquired. Jesus replied, 'Don't murder. Don't screw around. Don't steal and don't lie. Look after the old folks and look out for your neighbour's interests like you'd look out for your own.' 'Gee, I've done all that,' the man replied. 'What more do I need to do?' Jesus replied, 'If you really want to get your act together, go and sell your property and give all the proceeds to the poor . . . and come follow me.' When the young man heard what Jesus said, he turned away in terrible distress because he had a lot of property and didn't want to part with it.

Then Jesus said to his followers, 'It is extremely difficult for the affluent to be a part of the movement. In fact, it's easier to get a fully loaded truck through the keyhole of a welfare apartment than it is to get a wealthy person to be a part of God's movement among the poor.' When the followers of Jesus heard this, they freaked out. 'Who of us can make it then?' 'Humanly speaking,' Jesus said, 'it is impossible. But with God anything is possible.' Peter said, 'We've left everything to follow you. What's in it for us?' Jesus reassured him, 'When the True Leader comes into his own, you will have an important part in the organisation. Everyone who has given up property or relationships for the sake of my cause will go through a tough time, but they will get more than enough to meet their needs. Just remember. Many who are first now will be last then, and many who are last now will be first then!'

Matthew 19:16–30

2   What was the man's question?
3   How would we have answered him?
4   When the man claimed to be good, Jesus did not counter his claim. Instead, he pointed out, he was not good enough. What was required of him to be really good?
5   Why do we imagine Jesus answered him this way? Why was it necessary for him to give his wealth to the poor for him to be really good?
6   Why do we think Jesus considered this rich young aristocrat was sinning by hanging on to his wealth? Was it that his money had become his god? Was he refusing to take action that could redress injustice? Was it both of these? Or something else again?
7   Do we consider that we are rich?
8   Riches are relative. How do we normally measure whether we are rich or not?
9   Compared to the poverty of the majority of the world's population, do we think Jesus could look at us as rich or poor? How does this make us feel?
10 Why do we think Jesus said it is humanly impossible for the rich to give up their wealth and share it with the poor?
11 Why do we think Jesus stuck to his guns over the radical demands of his agenda, instead of making it easier by demanding less?
12 In what ways do we try to moderate the radical demands that Jesus makes on us through this story?

13 If Jesus told us that for us to be really good we must follow this same radical agenda, how would we react?

14 How do we imagine that God might enable us to follow this radical agenda, if we were willing to?

15 What security did Jesus offer to those who risked everything to take his radical agenda seriously?

16 Do we know of anyone who has taken this radical agenda to heart? Let's share their story with the group.

Action

Let's close our eyes and imagine Jesus standing in front of us, telling us to abandon our affluence and follow him. Let's ask God to help us to follow this command. As a sign of our seriousness let's take all the money we have in ur pockets and put it on the table. Let's then prayerfully choose one way that we can share our resources with those who need them more than us. Let's not tell everyone about what we intend to do, but let's tell at least one person, and report back to them when we have done what we have said we will do. On the way out we can pick up the money we put on the table, and either give it to someone else to help them with their project, or keep it to spend on the project that we have got in mind.

The revolutionary programme

(Requirements - paper and pen, a metal bowl and a box of matches)

Discussion

1 Let's start by writing out our hate list—of people who hate us, and people we hate.

2 Then read the following 'revolutionary principles' Jesus spelled out to people:

Love those who hate you, and be kind to those who would like to kill you. Bless those who curse you and pray for the welfare of those who frustrate you. Even if they beat you up, embrace them. Even if they rip you off, help them out. If someone needs something, give it to them. Don't try to get back anything they take. Treat others just as you would like them to treat you.

Luke 6:27–31

3 What is the difference between the way we usually act and the way Jesus suggests we ought to act?
4 How do we feel about Jesus' programme? Why?
5 What difference do we think it would make to our world if people followed this programme? Why?
6 What human principle is the programme based on?
7 Do we think we treat this principle as a cliché or do we use it as a guideline for the way that we actually relate to others?
8 What are some common circumstances where we could put this programme into operation and what effect do we think it would have?
9 Read the following further revolutionary principles Jesus spelled out to people:

If you love those who love you—big deal! Everybody does that. If you do good to those who do good to you, where's the grace in that? Everybody acts that way already. If you give with the expectation of getting something back, you're just doing business as usual. Love those who hate you. Do good to those who are bad to you. Give yourself fully and freely without any expectations of getting anything back. Then you'll have something to be really pleased about. Your actions will reflect the character of God. Because God is kind to all, the grateful and the ungrateful, saint and sinner alike.

Luke 6:32–36

10 Why does Jesus dismiss our efforts to be nice as being of no real significance?
11 What does Jesus suggest will be the only way we can make a significant difference to our society?
12 What is the divine principle on which the programme is based?
13 Why is this principle so revolutionary?

Action

Let's think of someone who is giving us a hard time. Let's pray for them, not cursing them, but blessing them. Then let's talk about how we can return good for the evil they do to us. And when we have finished, let's take our hate lists and burn them one by one in the metal bowl before we go.

The bloody struggle

(Requirements - paper and pen, two or three pictures of modern martyrs, like Dietrich Bonhoeffer, Martin Luther King, Oscar Romero etc.)

Discussion

1 Read about 'the bloody struggle' to which Jesus calls us:

Do not imagine that I have come to bring tranquillity. I have not come to bring a gin and tonic, but a gun. For I have come to put people in conflict with each other—even in their own family. Anyone who cares more for their parents than they care for me and my cause, doesn't deserve to be a part of the movement. Anyone

who cares more for their children than they care for me and my cause, doesn't deserve to be part of the movement. Anyone who wants to follow in my footsteps but is not willing to face the firing squad, is not good enough for me. Anyone who tries to preserve their life will waste it, but anyone who wastes their life for me and my movement will preserve the spirit that makes life worth living.
Matthew 10:34–39

2   What does the gun (or a 'sword' in the original) stand for?
3   How do we react to the statement that Jesus has not come to bring a gin and tonic but a gun?
4   What kind of conflict does Jesus say the struggle will involve?
5   How do we feel about such conflicts, even if they are for the sake of a good cause? Why?
6   Elsewhere Jesus says we must take care of our families, so what does he mean when he says that anyone who cares more for their parents or their children than they care for him or his cause doesn't deserve to be a part of the movement?
7   What does the firing squad ('crucifixion' in the original) stand for?
8   In the conflict Jesus envisaged, he talks about bringing a gun, not using a gun; facing a firing squad, not forming a firing squad; dying, not killing. What does this tell us about the conduct he expects from those involved in the struggle for love and justice?
9   Why can we expect that those who struggle for love and justice will face conflict and suffering?
10 What are some contemporary examples of those who have set aside security, safety and comfort to become involved in the bloody struggle for love and justice, and ultimately faced the 'firing squad'?
11 Place the pictures of the modern martyrs, such as Dietrich Bonhoeffer, Martin Luther King, and Oscar Romero on the table.

12 In what ways are they models for the way we should follow
    Jesus in the ongoing struggle?
13 Are we willing to join them in the ongoing struggle?
14 What may be the consequences if we do?
15 What are the consequences if we don't?
16 What do we think Jesus meant when he concluded by saying,
    'Anyone who tries to preserve their life will waste it, but anyone
    who wastes their life for me and my movement will preserve
    the spirit that makes life worth living'?

Action

Let's think of an issue of love and justice, where, if we stood up and
were counted, conflict would be created. Let's share this with the
rest of the group and then allow the group to pray for us, asking
God to give us the courage to face that anticipated conflict. Maybe
the issue we want to take a stand on provokes a strong reaction
from other people in our group. If so, let's take time to talk with
one another, listen to one another's views, and pray that God will
give us all wisdom and strength for the struggle.

Over coffee, let's discuss how, as a group, we may be able to
stand with each other and encourage each other to work for love
and justice in the face of a possible violent backlash.

The mustard seed conspiracy

(Requirements - paper and pen, a packet of mustard seeds)

Discussion

1 What do we think we can achieve in terms of real change in society?
2 How do we feel when we are so small compared to the big
   forces that we are up against?

3 Read the following short statements about the mustard seed conspiracy:

The mustard seed is the smallest seed of them all, yet when it grows it is the biggest tree in the garden. Its branches become a haven for wild birds to build their nests.
 Matthew 13:31

4 Pass around the packet of mustard seeds, making sure everyone gets a seed.
5 Why do we think Jesus uses a tiny seed to symbolise our efforts?
6 Why doesn't Jesus consider small efforts insignificant?
7 What reasons do we have for believing that the smallest effort might in the long run be of the greatest significance?
8 How can we encourage one another to live as if the smallest efforts can be of the greatest significance?
9 What examples do we know of people whose efforts appeared to have very little significance, yet in the end turned out to be of great significance to society?
10 What does the picture of a tiny seed becoming a tree where wild birds build their nests, convey to us?
11 How can we use this imagery of trees and nests to evaluate the effectiveness of our efforts?
12 What has to happen to the seed before it becomes a tree?

Action

Let's think of one way we can bury ourselves in the lives of the community. Let's share our decision with someone else. Then, let's take a mustard seed in our hand and pray that our 'mustard seed' effort may blossom into a 'tree of refuge' for those in trouble.

C   Resources that can Inform the Heart

There is nothing in this book I did not beg or borrow—if not steal—from others, including my wife, my parents, my children, my brothers and sisters, my friends and my fellow-workers, and a whole range of people whom I have never met, yet to whom I owe so much. I would recommend a range of literature which might be as valuable to you as it has been for me in developing a spirituality for a servant church in contemporary society.

Jesus Before Christianity (Darton, Longman & Todd, 1977) by Albert Nolan, is an excellent introduction to a contemporary encounter with the person of Christ, in contrast to Christianity as a religion. The two classic texts on the person of Christ by William Barclay, called *The Mind of Jesus* (SCM,1960), and *Crucified and Crowned* (SCM, 1961) are as refreshing today as the day they were written. Philip Yancey's *The Jesus I Never Knew* (Zondervan,1995) is a wonderful modern portrait of the carpenter from Nazareth who has become the central reference point for charting the path of human progress.

The Upside Down Kingdom (Herald Press, 2003*)* by Donald B. Kraybill is a study of the way of Christ which provides practical guidance for a Christ-like engagement with the world around about us. *The Politics of Jesus* (Eerdmans,1994), by John Howard Yoder, is a seminal book on the personal, social and political ethics of Christ-like community. *Life on the Road* (Lancer, 1992) and *The Fringes of Freedom* (Lancer, 1990), by Athol Gill, help us take the insights of Christ out of the gospels and apply them to our neighbourhood.

The Community of the Spirit (Herald Press,1993), by Norman Kraus, is an excellent text on the passionate altruistic character of the pentecostal apostolic community. In *Paul's Idea of Community* (Hendrickson, 1994), Robert Banks presents a theological interpretation of community, looking at the early house churches in their historical setting; while in *The Church Comes Home: Building Community and Mission through Home Churches* (Hendrickson, 1998), Robert and Julia Banks translate the meaning of their theological interpretation of community into the way in which we can live out the mission of the church today. *Catch the Wind* (Regent College, 2003), by Charles Ringma, explores the process of deconstructing and reconstructing the church, so as to develop models of church 'as if people mattered.'

Many of us are uncertain how to cultivate a spiritual life which is vital and relevant. In *Celebration of Discipline* (Hodder & Stoughton, 1999), Richard Foster shows how the classical disciplines of meditation, prayer, study, simplicity, solitude, submission, service, confession, worship, guidance and celebration can continue to promote the courage and joy to engage our world which we need today. In *Money, Sex and Power* (Hodder & Stoughton, 2000), Richard Foster illustrates how we can respond to the dominating issues in modern society authentically and creatively.

Just about any book written by Henri Nouwen and Jean Vanier is worth reading. But if I were to recommend one book by Henri Nouwen, it would be *Life Of The Beloved* (Crossroad, 2002). It's about how we can develop the art of spiritual living in a secular world. And if my wife were to recommend one book by Jean Vanier, it would be *Community And Growth* (St. Paul, 1979). It's about how we can develop the art of community living in a competitive world. Both these books, full of painful reflections from living in community with marginalised and disadvantaged people, have sustained Ange and me in our struggle. *The Church and Community Development* by George Lovell (Grail Publications, 1972) is an excellent account of practical methods that the church can use in its work in the community. *Human and Religious Factors in Church and Community Work* (Grail Publications, 1982), also by George Lovell, is an honest evaluation of the strengths and weaknesses of the practical methods that the church can use in its work in the community.

A Practical Guide To A Community Ministry (Westminster, 1993) by David Bos, helps us to explore local, social, ecumenical processes in developing church-based community-focused ministries; while *Caring For The Least* (Herald,1992) by David Caes, provides us with plenty of stories, written by poor people, and those who work with them, that help us escape the wealth trap, connect with poor neighbours, break through social and cultural stereotypes, and take constructive action together.

Comfortable Compassion? Poverty, Power and the Church (Paulist Press, 1987) by Charles Elliot is an excellent reflection on the changes of consciousness we have to make. *Transforming Power* (IVP, 2003) by Robert C. Linthicum, subtitled *Biblical Strategies for Making a Difference in Your Community*, is also very helpful. *Walking with the Poor* (Orbis Books, 1999) by Bryant Myers and *Working with the Poor* (MARC, 1999), edited by Myers, are two brilliant books which embody integral transformational ministry in both rich and poor societies.

Last but not least, is *Servants Among The Poor* (OMF, 1998) by Jenni M.Craig. This book is a moving account of a heroic effort to incarnate the gospel in the slums of Asia. It is an inspiring story, but it is definitely *not* triumphalistic. It documents the dogged struggle of Servants, through wonderful successes and awful failures, as they try to figure out how to do holistic community development with the poorest of the poor in the Philippines.

D Courses that can Transform the Heart

There are two courses that we offer that can help you in your practice of Christ-like community work. The first is *With Christ in the Community,* a two week course run in West End, Brisbane, Australia. The second is *Compassionate Community Work,* an extension course that uses *Not Religion But Love* as a text and that you can study anywhere in the world.

1 With Christ in the Community

For the last twenty years, twice a year, we have run courses in Brisbane that we call 'With Christ in the Community'. These are courses for people who want an intensive introduction to a Christ-centred approach to community development work with disadvantaged groups of people who are living in the city. The courses are run for two weeks mid-year, usually the last week of June to the first week of July, and three weeks at the end of the year, usually the three weeks leading up to Christmas. The course involves living in our neighbourhood, West End, with some people from the West End Waiters' Union.

The course includes spiritual disciplines, corporate reflections, practical service, holistic evangelism, cross-cultural mission, cooperative organisation, and nonviolent action. The costs of the course are decided by the participants in a group cost-sharing workshop, that we run as part of the course. People pay anything from

$100 to $250 per week, usually between $150 and $200, for accommodation, meals and tuition combined. People come to the course from all over Australia, and from other parts of the world as well. All are welcome.

Lyn and Steve Hatfield-Dodds describe what the course is like. 'The daily program started around 6:30 am with prayer—experimenting with new ways of encountering Christ, and getting a feel for what it might be like to work with him in the local community. After breakfast we joined in studies drawn from the gospels, focusing on Christ, and what it means for us to become more Christ-like. In the latter part of the morning [people] shared of their life in the local community—involved in peace networks, community arts, housing assistance, legal aid, refugee resettlement, and offering hospitality and shelter to those without a place to stay. The afternoons were unstructured times, to allow us to get to know the neighbourhood, and its people. In the evenings we had dinner with different members of the network. Most days finished with a much-needed briefing session. We also managed to squeeze in time to deliver meals on wheels, go on outings [with people who were intellectually disabled], and help out at an evening meal for over a hundred homeless men.'

'The nine of us on the course lived in a group house for the first week, moving out to stay in boarding houses or hostels we found for ourselves in the second week. For many of us this was a difficult and sometimes frightening experience, living in the midst of depressed and often violent lives, and it was good to come back together for the last few days to the security of group living. Highlights of the course for us [included] being involved in a Murri service in a maximum security prison; hearing people's stories; developing friendships; [and] meeting people who not only talk about being Christ-like or compassionate, but who are trying to put these things into practice.'

We try to keep the numbers on our courses small in order to facilitate maximum participation in the course, and minimal impact, by the course, on the community, so if you are interested in coming to one of our courses, you would need to apply early to be sure to get a place. If you are interested in coming to one of our courses you can apply by writing to: 'With Christ In The Community' either by mail, PO Box 5519, West End, Brisbane, Queensland, Australia, 4101 or by email: dave@tear.org.au

For further information check out our web site, www.daveandrews.com.au

2   Compassionate Community Work

Compassionate Community Work is an introductory course in Christ-like community work. It can be studied formally as a subject for university or seminary, or informally at home in your own church or community.

Compassionate Community Work has an inner dimension and an outer dimension.

The inner dimension, or "soul", of the course is my passion for in-situ, spiritual, experiential, personal, relational, ethical, action-reflection community development education. It seeks to provide people with the opportunity to explore a dynamic spirituality that is essential for developing a healthy faith based community. The Trinity is the model, Christ is the example, the Gospel is the process, and the Spirit is the power for healthy faith-based community development.

After researching five different Christian communities in depth, sociologist Luther Smith wrote:

> The primary indicator of communal well-being is that members feel their fellowship approximates the qualities of a caring family. Hardship and failures will be the occasion for creative solutions and increased resolve. They do not break the spirit of a community. But loss of mutual respect and steadfast caring strikes a deathblow at the very heart of a community.[17]

It is my hope that this training will provide the opportunity to explore the sense of significance and solidarity which is at the heart of community. Hopefully through this learning experience, you will develop a sense of deep mutual respect with people around you—as in a 'healthy extended family'—in which you will be free to 'rejoice together and mourn together'.[18]

The outer dimension of the course deals with community development knowledge, skills, principles, practices and competencies, seeking to impart:

1) underpinning knowledge, such as:
   - the nature and the dynamics of community
   - community development principles and practices
   - community development strategies and tactics
   - methods for encouraging community participation
   - concepts of effective community leadership
   - organisational systems,
   - program guidelines
   - project budgets
   - funding options

2) underpinning skills, such as:
  · formal and informal networking
  · liaising with a range of people
  · researching community issues
  · developing community policies
  · facilitating community meetings
  · negotiating community agreements
  · preparing community budgets
  · promoting community activities
  · evaluating community programs
  · writing community reports

When you complete *Compassionate Community Work*, you will be able to:
  · demonstrate a developed understanding of community and community development in light of biblical material
  · articulate a broad understanding of general theories related to community and community development
  · analyse with insight the issues involved in doing church-based community development
  · identify and develop opportunities for church community leadership
  · appreciate Christian responses which enhance human dignity, community solidarity and effective witness
  · articulate and value the uniquely Christian contribution to community and community development

Compassionate Community Work includes processes, exercises, a set text, study notes, additional readings, and a simple series of community tasks that you can work through, step-by-step, in the context of your own community.

The course also includes a set of instructions to assist you in self-managed study. However, no course on community work could possibly be done in total isolation. So you will need a learning partner for this course. It doesn't matter if it is a new acquaintance or an old friend. It should be someone you believe you can work with, someone you feel comfortable with, you can collaborate with, and be accountable to.

A learning partner does not need to be present when you do most of the study sessions. But there are some sessions where it is absolutely essential that you have one or two learning partners with you, in order to be able to explore the subject being studied with integrity. The learning partners for these sessions need not be learning partners you have chosen for the whole course, but any helpful people who might be available.

At the end of each session, there are Community Tasks set for you to do.. These activities provide the that are the basis for the action and reflection at the heart of the course.

You are also encouraged to keep Working Notes of informal personal reflections on specific lessons you learn from this course, through your engagement with community development theory and practice in your community. Working Notes are not an objective reporting of events *per se*, but more subjective, personal reflections on some of the thoughts, feelings and issues that the course raises for you to consider.

While reading widely on the topic of community development is strongly encouraged, we have tried to provide enough resources for you to read without having to access a library. Additional articles and stories have been provided for you on my website www.daveandrews.com.au

References

1   Goleman, D. *Emotional Intelligence*, (New York: Bantam Books, 1995) p. 119

2   Goleman, pp. 328,329

3   Macmurray, J. *Freedom in the Modern World*, (London: Faber & Faber, 1958) pp. 28-29

4   Macmurray, p. 55

5   Macmurray, p. 88-90

6   Macmurray, p. 58–59

7   Macmurray, p. 65–70

8   Gandhi, M. *The Message of Jesus*, (Bombay: Bharitya Vidya Bhavan, 1971) foreword

9   Gandhi, p. 7

10 Gandhi, p. 111

11 Gandhi, afterword

12 Gandhi, p. 40, 79

13 Keen, S. *Fire in the Belly*, (New York: Bantam Books, 1991) 102

14 Keen, p. 246-268

15 Jung, C. 'The Development of Personality', *Collected Works*, (London: Routledge, Kegan, & Paul, 1953) pp. 167-187

16 adapted from *H. van der Looy, A Rule for a New Brother*, London: Darton, Longman & Todd, 1986.

17 Smith, L. *Intimacy and Mission* (Herald Press, 1994), pp. 98-100

18 *Research in Organisational Change and Development,* Vol 1 (JAI Press, 1987), pp. 129-169.

Also by Dave Andrews:

Christi-Anarchy

Published by Wipf and Stock Publishers

This is a courageous and provocative study, likely to earn applause from some, and brickbats from others, but certain to challenge and to stimulate serious reflection.

Dave Andrews attacks Christian complacency and calls us back to the non-violent, yet radically subversive 'Way' of Jesus.

Many of us who teach church history feel uncomfortable with facile explanations of its dark, demonic side.

This book confronts that darkness with a sobering accusation: post-Constantinian Christianity has so perverted the 'Way' that, far from being aberrations, atrocities have become its natural excrescences.

Christianity's reputation is so besmirched that a startling, new name is proposed for the humble, loving 'Way' of life taught and exemplified by Jesus.

Those afraid of moving out of their comfort zone are advised not to read this book!

Professor Patricia Harrison, PhD, Tabor College, Sydney, Australia

The long history of the project Christendom may be typified as the house of authority, with its many attendant abuses of power. But a different thread runs through history as well, based on the subversive memory of the early Jesus movement. This could be typified as the house of freedom.

Here welcome, hospitality, downward mobility, servant leadership, common purse, intentional community, peace and justice are the dancing residents.

In the tradition of Vernard Eller, Dave Andrews invites us to dwell in the house of freedom, and fling open all the doors and windows!

Professor Charles Ringma, PhD, Regent College, Vancouver, Canada

This book is a radical but loving reconstruction of the movement of Jesus Christ, in protest against its distortions.

Dave Andrews, one of the leading prophetic voices of our time, brings all of his passion and insight to bear in a way which will both disturb and inspire.

Christi-Anarchy has that uncomfortable air of a message crying out ot be heard, and I hope it is widely read.

Mike Riddell, author of *alt.spirit@metro.m3* and *Godzone*

15254231R00124

Printed in Great Britain
by Amazon